MBINED FORCES of FRANCE & SPAIN,

ith LORD NELSON, Cape Trafalgar, bearing E.S.E. 4 Leagues.

Spartiate

Minotaur

Orion

Ajax

Entreprenant
Cutter

Agamemnon

Phœbe
Britannia
Lord Northesk

Conqueror

Naiad

Leviathan

Pickle
Schooner

Neptune

Sirius

Africa

Temeraire

Euryalus

Victory
Lord Nelson

Colossus

Rayo

Neptuno

Formidable
RearAdmᵗ Dumanoir

Scipion

SᵗAugustino

Asis

Duguay Trouin

Mont Blanc

Heros

SᵗTrinidad
RearAdmᵗ Cisneros

Redoutable

Bucentaur
Admᵗ Villeneuve

Neptune

SᵗJusto

Leandro

Indomptable

SᵗAnna
ViceAdmᵗ D'Alava

Rhin

Hortance

Corncli

Furd Brig

Fougueux

L'Aigle

Montanez

wood

ign

isle

Thesues

Principe?

to its correctness by the Flag Officers of the Euryalus, & Admᵗ Villeneuve

ᵗ 1806, by Edwᵈ Orme, Printseller to the King, and Royal Family 59 Bond Street, London

NELSON
COMMEMORATED IN
GLASS PICTURES

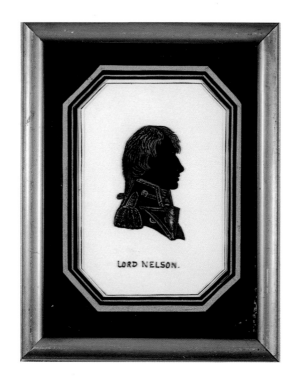

LORD NELSON.

by
L.P.Le QUESNE

with a foreword by
TOM POCOCK

ANTIQUE COLLECTORS' CLUB

ISBN 1 85149 396 4

British Library Cataloguing-in-Publication Data
A catalogue record for this book is available from the British Library

Printed in England
by the Antique Collectors' Club Ltd., Woodbridge, Suffolk

CONTENTS

The endpapers are reproduced from J. S. Corbett, *The Campaign of Trafalgar* (1910).

Two of the illustrations in this book (no. 4 and Figure A) are from the National Maritime Museum (www.nmm.ac.uk), from whose Picture Library (tel. 0208 312 6600/604) copies may be obtained. The Royal Naval Museum also has a website (www.royalnavalmuseum.org).

FOR
PADDY

FOREWORD

by Tom Pocock

The emotional impact of the death of Nelson at the Battle of Trafalgar has never been equalled amongst the British. Those who experienced it were often lost for words to describe the upsurge of grief and joy; this epic quality of triumph and tragedy has been a powerful element in British memory ever since.

No echo in this is more potent, or more poignant, than the subject of this book. The commemoration of Lord Nelson in glass pictures was an immediate reaction to the news from the heart and guts of the nation. Paintings on canvas or paper, engravings, statuary and ceramics were all to be used and developed in commemoration but none have the immediacy of the glass pictures.

Almost all of the pictures here described were produced within six months of the battle on 21 October 1805, and none after the following year, when the hero was buried in St. Paul's Cathedral. They came like a sob of grief that would mellow into the romantic sorrow expressed in other media, which continues to this day.

Raw emotion is only part of the appeal of these glass pictures. There is a touchingly naïve quality in their imagery, reflecting the imagination of the time. The first were made before details of Nelson's death had been published, so the artists imagined him expiring on a crimson sofa in his cabin, reclining on the quarterdeck or being caught in the arms of his officers. An alternative was the allegorical picture with Britannia, Fame, Neptune, airborne angels and assorted tritons and naiads riding in triumphal chariots fashioned from scallop shells and attended by dolphins and lions with white moustaches. After the apotheosis of Nelson came reportage of the lying in state, the aquatic cortège on the Thames and the great funeral itself.

The emotion captured by the images is brought alive by the glow of colours, with which the transferred drawings on the reverse of the glass were painted; the rich, strong colours, whether jubilant or sombre, remaining more vibrant in this medium than in any other. In the first study of this iconography, Leslie Le Quesne explains in fascinating detail the development of the glass picture, the technique of its production and, above all, its months of gloriously sentimental triumph nearly two centuries ago.

ACKNOWLEDGEMENTS

This book could not possibly have been compiled without the help of many friends and experts. I am particularly indebted to John May, an expert in the whole field of Nelson memorabilia, from whom over the years I have learnt much of what I know about glass pictures. I am also grateful to John Cox, whose wide knowledge of pictures and paper has extended my appreciation of the problems related to the production of these glass pictures. The expertise of Elizabeth Miller, Assistant Curator of Prints at the Victoria and Albert Museum, added a new dimension to my understanding of the nature of the prints used in making them, and I am deeply grateful to her for authoritative guidance.

Sadly, prudence prevents my naming the individuals who have kindly allowed me to photograph their Nelson glass pictures for inclusion in the catalogue, and it must suffice to say that I am indeed grateful to them. On my visits to the National Maritime Museum, Greenwich, and the Royal Naval Museum, Portsmouth, to view the pictures in their collections, I was greatly helped by the courtesy of their staff, to whom my thanks are extended. I am grateful to Mr Andrew Helme, Curator of the Nelson Museum, Monmouth, for the trouble which he took to enable me to see the collection of Nelson glass pictures there, and for permission to reproduce no. 70. I am also grateful to the Trustees of the National Maritime Museum for permission to reproduce no. 3 and Figure A, to the Dean and Chapter of St. Paul's for permission to reproduce, in Appendix II, the picture of Nelson's tomb, and to the London Topographical Society for permission to reproduce the map on page 103.

I owe a special debt of gratitude to Mr James Hobsley and to Mr Christopher Phillips for their skilled photography which produced all but a few of the illustrations which form such an important feature of the catalogue. Their pictures reproduce accurately the colours which are such a characteristic of the originals and capture their particular charm. I am indebted to my son William, who took a few of the pictures in unusual circumstances, and to my brother Laurence, who gave me valuable guidance in some of the finer historical points covered in the notes.

From the start of this project Lavinia and Richard Emanuel, friends of long standing, have constantly encouraged me with their enthusiastic interest: their cogent, knowledgeable comments, always expressed with delightful freedom, have been of inestimable help to me at all times, and for all this I am deeply in their debt. I am grateful to Colin White and Peter Warwick, who read the early text and helped me with constructive comments. Professor Christopher Elrington most kindly undertook the editorial responsibilities of turning a manuscript into a book, an act beyond the usual call of friendship, and it is a great pleasure to express my gratitude to him for his indefatigable, skilled help in producing this work in its final form.

Finally, adequate words are certainly lacking to express my gratitude to my late wife, Paddy. Indeed *une secrétaire particulière extraordinaire*, she not only typed the text many times without complaint, but was also solely responsible for the splendid, detailed reproduction of the caption to each picture, capturing so accurately the flavour of the period. Beyond this, she was my enthusiastic companion on most of the expeditions to view these pictures, and an invaluable critic at all stages, without whose aid I could not, and may well not, have completed the study.

November 2001   L. P. Le Quesne

INTRODUCTION

'When Nelson died it seemed as if no man was a stranger to another; for all were made acquaintances in the rights of a common anguish'

S. T. Coleridge[1]

Nelson was the first great national hero, and the grief at his death equalled the rejoicing for the victory of Trafalgar. Unknown to the public prior to his heroic deeds at the Battle of Cape St. Vincent in February 1797, Nelson established his fame by his overwhelming victory over the French eighteen months later at the Battle of the Nile. To mark this victory a great number of commemorative prints, mugs, plates etc. were produced glorifying Nelson and his achievement. For the remainder of his short life Nelson was a national hero, no aspect of his life being immune to public interest and gossip. The Battle of Copenhagen did not arouse the public acclaim of the Nile (see page 28, note ii) and, apart from three glass pictures (nos. 2-4 below), few prints, if any, or other memorabilia were produced.

As Nelson embarked at Portsmouth on his way to Trafalgar he remarked to Hardy 'I had their huzzas before, I have their hearts now.'[2] The truth of this was shown by the outpouring of grief throughout the nation which greeted the news of his death on 21 October 1805, in the hour of victory. In the weeks and months following this event a torrent of prints, engraved glass, mugs and plates of all types, fans, enamelled and brass boxes and a variety of other memorabilia were produced to commemorate the hero, the greatest number being various types of ceramic wares, decorated with prints, mouldings and colours applied in various ways. The production of these many forms of commemorative ware did not cease within a few months of Nelson's death, but has continued ever since, with bursts of activity to mark special dates, such as the centenary of his death, and there will surely be a flood of new pieces to mark the Trafalgar bicentenary in 2005.

Across this extensive field of Nelson memorabilia there is, as would be expected, a wide range in the standard of craftsmanship. Thus some of the early nineteenth century glass goblets and the rare enamel ware, and some of the early twentieth century ceramic ware, such as the Royal Doulton pieces, are of a very high standard. In contrast other pieces, produced in considerable numbers and designed for a much less wealthy stratum of society are, not surprisingly, of a lower order of workmanship. An altogether different and very interesting

[1] Quoted in O. M. W. Warner, *A Portrait of Lord Nelson* (1958), p. 358.
[2] T. Pocock, *Horatio Nelson* (1987), p. 316.

comparison applies to the two types of Nelson commemoratives which form coherent groups within the whole complex range, namely the glass pictures and the Staffordshire figures. Both types were originally made for the popular end of the market, but are now rare and much sought after. Both were produced by small groups of artisans, potters and printers, each clustered in a small area, one in London, the other in Staffordshire, but they differ, interestingly, in the time of their production in relation to Nelson's death, in their purpose and in their social significance.

Excluding the five pictures published before Trafalgar and the Treaty pictures (see page 16), most of the surviving glass pictures were published within six months of the battle (see page 20, Table 2). The earliest pictures of the death of Nelson (nos. 17-19) were published on 21 November, just fourteen days after the Gazette announcing Nelson's death at the Battle of Trafalgar had been published in London (see page 40, note iii). There are no known such pictures published after December 1806. In contrast with practically all other types of Nelson memorabilia, these pictures are unique in being produced solely during this short period, indicating that they should be looked on as a direct, authentic reflection of the widespread grief caused by the news of Nelson's death at Trafalgar. In their naïve fashion many of them were clearly intended to be a realistic picture of the event illustrated, while others of a monumental and allegorical nature reflect the depth of the adulation for Nelson and the grief at his death. In contrast the Staffordshire figures were made much later than the glass pictures, most of them probably being produced in the years 1840-60. It has been suggested by Gordon Pugh[1] that these figures were made at this time in response to renewed interest in Nelson resulting from the erection of the Nelson Column in Trafalgar Square, started in 1839 and finished in 1844. While there may be substance in this suggestion, it seems altogether more probable that other, more general factors were responsible, for at this time more figures of both Wellington and Napoleon were produced than of Nelson, and many more of Queen Victoria and Prince Albert. The Staffordshire figures of Nelson and the Death of Nelson (save for the jug busts of Nelson), in contrast to the Representational Glass Pictures, were clearly not intended as accurate representations of Nelson, rather their prime importance was decorative, as emphasised by the varying bright colouring given to his breeches. In the middle years of the nineteenth century a vast range of Staffordshire figures was sold widely throughout the country, reflecting the greater ease of transport and, with the boom in house-building and growing prosperity, the increasing demand for household ornaments. Prominent among these ornaments were the Staffordshire figures, notably the characteristic chimney pieces. While the Staffordshire figures of Nelson constitute an important and interesting component of Nelson memorabilia, it is against this background that they should be viewed, rather than as a direct expression of grief at his death.

There is an admirable review of the whole field of Nelson Commemoratives by John May,[2] a leading authority on the subject. Gordon Pugh's *Naval Ceramics* gives a profusely illustrated account of the topic, with a chapter devoted to Nelson

[1] P. D. Gordon Pugh, *Staffordshire Figures of the Victorian Era* (2nd edn. 1987), p. C222.
[2] In *The Nelson Companion*, ed. Colin White (1995), chapter 4.

and his Captains.[1] Similarly, John and Jennifer May's *Commemorative Pottery*, although covering a wider field, has a comprehensive, well-illustrated chapter on Naval and Military People and Events.[2] The whole subject of Staffordshire portrait figures has been extensively covered in a number of scholarly publications, notably by Thomas Balston;[3] by Anthony Oliver;[4] and by Gordon Pugh.[5] A. and N. Harding have reproduced magnificent colour pictures of over 2,900 such figures.[6]

Surprisingly little, however, has been written about commemorative glass pictures, and there is no catalogue of the Nelson glass pictures. Given their fragile nature, with the passing of the years the compilation of such a catalogue will become increasingly difficult and this book seeks to fill the gaps while it is still possible.

GLASS PICTURES

Glass pictures are not the same as glass paintings. In glass paintings, which were mainly imported from China in the eighteenth century, the paint was applied directly to the reverse side of a piece of glass.[7] In contrast, glass pictures are transfers of a black and white print on to the back of a piece of glass, the transfer then being painted over from the back in colour. Probably first described in Germany in 1669 by Johannes Kunckel[8] and popular particularly in France and Germany throughout the eighteenth century, the technique of making glass pictures was closely related to the development of mezzotints, and in particular to the desire to add colour to mezzotint prints.

The method by which glass pictures were made was, in essence, simple. Initially the print was soaked in water for four or five hours to remove the sizing from the paper, then laid flat between cloths and pressed gently to remove the excess water. It was then laid face down on a sheet of glass previously cut to size and covered with a layer of Venetian turpentine to act as an adhesive or cement, great care being taken to prevent any bubbles of air being trapped between the print and the turpentine. When completely dry the paper was again wetted, and rubbed gently with finger tips to remove the paper from the glass, 'leaving … the whole of the

[1] P. D. Gordon Pugh, *Naval Ceramics* (1971), chapter 2.

[2] John and Jennifer May, *Commemorative Pottery* (1972), chapter 3.

[3] Thomas Balston, *Staffordshire Portrait Figures of the Victorian Age* (1958).

[4] Anthony Oliver, *The Victorian Staffordshire Figure* (1971).

[5] Above, p. 10, note 1.

[6] A. and N. Harding, *Victorian Staffordshire Figures 1835-1875* (1998). The Nelson figures are in Volume One.

[7] C. L. Crossman, *The Decorative Arts of the China Trade* (1991), pp. 203-19.

[8] J. Kunckel, *Ars Vitrialis Experimentalis* (1669), quoted in Ann Massing, 'From Print to Painting: the Technique of Glass Transfer Painting', *Print Quarterly*, vol. 6 (1989), p. 385.

ink of the print upon the cement, and glass, in the same manner as if the original impression had been made there; by which method a complete drawing of the picture designed is obtained on the glass.'[1] Three or four further layers of turpentine or varnish were then applied to the back of the glass. When the last of these was dry the print was ready for painting over, with oil paint, the areas of paint being applied in the reverse order to that of normal painting.

The technique of making glass pictures was introduced into England in the last quarter of the seventeenth century, and it seems certain that the first person to produce and publish glass pictures in England was John Smith, a skilled engraver who worked closely with Godfrey Kneller, the leading portrait painter of the day. Very probably the first such picture was a portrait of Queen Mary, published in 1699 or 1700 from a mezzotint published in 1699.[2] Glass pictures were made widely in Germany, France and England throughout the eighteenth century, using mezzotint prints of pictures by the foremost artists of the day. During this period numerous descriptions of the technique were published, all essentially similar though differing in details.

The method of making flat sheets of glass was unknown in the eighteenth century, and the glass used for these pictures was Crown or Bristol glass. This was produced by blowing a large bubble of glass, cutting it open, and spreading it out as flat as possible. By this method it was not possible to make a completely flat sheet of glass, so that a characteristic of eighteenth and early nineteenth century glass pictures is that they are slightly curved, and this, together with its thinness, makes the glass of these pictures easily broken (see nos. 2, 4 and 70).

In England, throughout the eighteenth century a large number of fine glass pictures were produced, almost certainly entirely in London. In the early years, these pictures were without exception portraits, particularly of members of the royal family. In the later years decorative sets of the Four Continents, the Four Seasons and other similar subjects were produced, as well as a number of fine pictures of distinguished admirals. Made from mezzotint prints of high quality, these pictures were essentially works of fine art, designed for and purchased by wealthy gentry, and only a small number of each was made. In the latter half of the century, surely to satisfy the tastes of a less sophisticated, less wealthy section of society, a different type of glass picture began to appear, made from prints of less high quality with subjects of more popular appeal. Towards the end of the century an altogether simpler type of glass picture appeared. Produced in greater numbers than the earlier ones and based not on pure mezzotints but on simpler prints, at least partly etched (see Appendix I), and painted in bold colours, they have, in the words of John May, 'a basic interest and a naïve charm'.[3] Many of these pictures

[1] R. Dossie, *The Handmaid to the Arts* (1758), pp. 325-6.
[2] J. May, in *Antiques and Art Weekly*, vol. 12 (1973), no. 4, p. 28.
[3] J. May, in *Collectors' Guide*, Jan. 1972, p. 49.

were produced to commemorate important contemporary events and people. May, an authority on this commemorative type of glass picture, says that the first such picture that he has seen 'records the surrender of Tippoo Sahib's two sons to Lord Cornwallis, as hostages to his good behaviour, in 1792', and that the earliest naval picture, a very rare one, commemorates the Battle of Camperdown, in 1797. There were a number of pictures recording the trials and tribulations of members of the royal family, but the greatest number were devoted to the death of Nelson. There were only a few glass pictures of Wellington, no doubt reflecting the fact that Wellington was never a great popular hero in the same sense as Nelson. The last known commemorative glass picture was one 'regretting the death of Queen Caroline', but ones of religious subjects continued to be produced in diminishing numbers for another thirty years.[1]

All the known Nelson glass pictures were made and published by a number of small firms in London, mostly clustered together in an area north and west of Smithfield. The small streets and lanes in which most of them were situated, Cow Lane and Fox and Knot (sometimes Fork and Not) Court, have largely disappeared but are marked on maps of Georgian London.[2] Several of the firms can be found recorded in the Post Office Directory (see page 19, Table 1), though it is to be noted that Hinton, who published more of the Nelson pictures than anyone else, is not mentioned in the directory. All had disappeared by the middle of the century.[3] It is not known where the pictures were made, but it is of interest that the four firms publishing Nelson pictures and recorded in the directory all give as their trade one closely involved in the picture, print or another aspect of the glass trade. It may be that as well as publishing the glass pictures the firms also produced them, at least in part. If not, it is certain that they were made close by, for this area of London was the centre of the craft trades. The pictures were sold in black wooden frames, usually simply grooved and beaded, sometimes partially gilded, and occasionally covered with a thin layer of brass. Because of their fragile nature the great majority of these pictures are still found in their original frames. For the same reason, because of the risk of damage in transport, it is probable that nearly all were sold in London.

The only modern book devoted to the subject of glass pictures is *The Story of Old English Glass Pictures, 1690-1810* (1928), by H.G. Clarke. This book is mainly concerned with earlier glass pictures made from mezzotints, and Clarke clearly disapproves of the less sophisticated type of picture, such as those of Nelson, which he dismisses as 'coarsely-executed and poorly-coloured examples of the art, produced in the early nineteenth century. Collectors will be wise to exclude such pictures altogether.'[4]

In his articles on Glass Transfer Pictures, Winkworth gives a standard description of the eighteenth century technique of making these pictures. Most of these two articles are concerned with glass pictures of eighteenth century mezzotint prints. Like Clarke he is dismissive of the simpler nineteenth century pictures, ending up 'in conclusion a word must be said … about these decadent examples, mostly a product of the nineteenth century, which may be described as the final flicker of

---

[1] J. May, 'The Secret behind Glass-Painting' [sic], *Art and Antiques*, vol. 12.4 (1973), pp. 28-31.
[2] *The A to Z of Georgian London* (London Topographical Society, publ. no. 126, 1982), pl. 4, of which part is reproduced here, page 103.
[3] The Fine Arts Trade Guild has no record of any of these firms in its archives, which go back to 1847.
[4] Clarke, *Old English Glass Pictures*, p. 4.

our eighteenth century rushlight. These are the coarsest of prints, ill drawn and poorly painted, the subjects mostly patriotic or scriptural, the 'Death of Nelson' being perhaps the most painfully persistent.'[1]

In contrast to the articles by Winkworth, the two articles by John May[2] give clear accounts of how glass pictures were made and their development in style through the eighteenth and early nineteenth century, while giving particular attention to these pictures so derided by Clark and Winkworth. There is a scholarly review of the whole subject of glass pictures by Ann Massing, with copious references to the earlier literature.[3]

NELSON GLASS PICTURES

This catalogue describes the seventy Nelson glass pictures which the author has been able to identify. These pictures have been inspected in public galleries and, principally, in private collections. The total of seventy pictures consists of fifty-nine either of or directly concerned with Nelson, four related to his battles (nos. 2, 3, 20, 21) and seven Treaty pictures (nos. 64-70), containing representations of or referral to Nelson in pictures celebrating peace treaties. The pictures are of two sizes, the larger (forty-nine pictures) measuring 13¾ x 9⅞in (35 x 25cm), the smaller (twenty-one pictures) 9½ x 7½in (24 x 19cm). In most the long axis of the picture is horizontal, but in twenty it is vertical. Across the bottom of each picture there is a strip, up to 1⅜in (3.5cm) deep, on which is printed the title of the picture, usually quite brief, but sometimes a relatively long sentence, a striking feature of the titles being the variety of print used in a single caption. Across the very bottom of the picture is printed the name, with the address, of the publisher and the date of publication. Because of the curvature of the glass, the pictures do not fit tightly in the frames, with the result that in some the picture slips down in the frame obscuring the information about the publisher: gentle shaking may shift the picture enough to enable it to be read, but this is not always possible, and because of the risk of damaging the picture by removing it from the frame it is wise in such instances to accept that the publisher remains unknown.

[1] S. Winkworth, 'Glass Transfer Pictures', *Apollo* (1926), pp. 147-50, 224-7.
[2] 'Don't Let the Char do the Dusting', in *Collectors' Guide*, Jan. 1972; 'The Secret behind Glass-Painting', in *Art and Antiques Weekly* (1973). There is a further, slighter article on these pictures by John Woodiwiss, 'Glass Pictures', in *House and Garden*, Feb. 1963.
[3] 'From Print to Painting: the Technique of Glass Transfer Painting', in *Print Quarterly*, vol. 6 (1989), pp. 383-98.

The figure of seventy different glass pictures concerned with Nelson cannot be taken as representing the definitive number of such pictures actually produced. One of the pictures included below (no. 2) had not been seen by the author until shortly after the text of the book had gone to the publisher. Further, in *Remembering Nelson*, the catalogue of the Lily Lambert McCarthy Collection at the Royal Naval Museum, Portsmouth, Figs. 32 and 33 reproduce two prints of Nelson at the Nile. The first, entitled 'The HAZARDS of WAR, or, NELSON WOUNDED', shows Nelson standing shortly after being wounded, supported on either side, with blood pouring down from a wound in his left [*sic*] brow. The second, entitled 'The REWARD of COURAGE, or, NELSON TRIUMPHANT', shows Nelson seated on a couch in the stern cabin of the *Vanguard*, with the French Admiral Blanquet presenting him with his colours. Both pictures were published by Fairburn on 24 November 1798. In style these two prints are characteristic of those used in the making of many Nelson glass pictures. This is particularly so in the case of the second, in which the fanciful reconstruction of Nelson's cabin is in many respects similar to that in no. 19, suggesting that the same artist might have been responsible for both. So, given that the two prints reproduced in *Remembering Nelson* are similar in all respects to those used in making glass pictures, and that their publisher, Fairburn, is known to have published at least two glass pictures of Nelson (nos. 2 and 3), it is tempting to speculate that three years earlier he may have made two others – which await discovery. If so they will be the earliest Nelson glass pictures published, and the only two of Nelson at the Battle of the Nile. (See also note ii to nos. 46 and 47.) Moreover, it is of interest to note that three of the pictures (nos. 2, 4 and 70) were seen only in pieces, emphasising the fragility of these pictures, and raising the possibility that all the copies of some less popular pictures may have been broken. (See also page 17 and note to no. 36.)

In the great majority of instances there is no difficulty in distinguishing one picture from another, the individuality of a picture being established not only by differences in the actual print but also by differences in the title, name of publisher and date of publication. These latter features almost invariably resolve any difficulty, but rarely the distinction may depend upon individual judgement as to whether or not the pictures were made from separate prints. Thus nos. 17 and 18 were both published by Hinton on 21 November 1805, and the central group of Nelson and the three officers around him are identical, but no. 18 contains such important additions, in the figures on the poop and the additional figures on the deck, that it must have been made from a different print and hence is catalogued separately. Similarly, in nos. 61 and 62, both published by Stampa on the same date, the central group of Nelson, Neptune and the sea-horses are identical, but no. 61 contains, on the right, an additional figure and is on this ground catalogued as a separate picture. Colour is of no significance in establishing the individuality of a picture, for the painting of the print, the last stage in its production, was a relatively unskilled task and it is clear that some discretion was left to the artist, with the result that it is not uncommon to find examples of markedly different colouring of the same print.

The seventy pictures fall into four distinct groups: Representational, thirty-six pictures (nos. 1-36); Monumental, fourteen pictures (nos. 37-50); Allegorical, thirteen pictures (nos. 51-63); Treaty, seven pictures (nos. 64-70).

The Representational Pictures portray an individual, such as Nelson in no. 1, or actual events, such as Nelson's battles (nos. 2, 3, 21), his fatal wound (e.g. no. 9) or his funeral – there being five pictures of his funeral barge (nos. 24-28) and six of the funeral car (nos. 29-34). Some of these pictures, such as nos. 1, 2 and 3, three pre-Trafalgar pictures, are of a higher standard than most, in which the draughtsmanship and design are essentially crude. The pictures of the barge and funeral car, though differing in several minor respects, clearly give, in broad terms, an accurate picture of these two important components of the magnificent funeral, but the pictures in which the artist had to rely essentially on his imagination, such as Nelson receiving his fatal wound, are altogether cruder. Nonetheless, there is a compelling charm about these undoubtedly naïve pictures, such as the highly imaginative picture of the dying Nelson (no. 19). He is depicted lying on a comfortable couch, with weeping officers at either end, and the surgeon to the *Victory*, William Beatty, in spotless white trousers, kneeling by his side. The surgeon is counting Nelson's pulse, with the dying man's wrist in one hand and a turnip watch in the other.

The Monumental Pictures are all basically similar in design, consisting of either a bust of Nelson on a plinth or a portrait of Nelson on the side of the plinth, in each case suitably inscribed, with flags on either side and appropriate figures of weeping sailors, Britannia, Fame etc. The finest, most delicate of these monumental pictures, more complex in its design than the others, is no. 44, with its smaller version, no. 45.

The Allegorical Pictures. In these pictures it is the dying Nelson himself, not a bust or portrait of him, to whom the mythical figures of Britannia, Fame etc. express their grief either as he dies in the arms of Victory or as they accompany him to shore in a fantastical wheeled chariot drawn by sea horses. Crude as they are in artistic terms and, to our taste, expressing an excessive adulation for the dying hero, these pictures should not be construed as reflecting emotions confined at that time to the less sophisticated strata of society. Essentially the same response to Nelson's death is reflected in the later, technically utterly different, but hugely popular pictures, the 'Immortality of Nelson', by Benjamin West, and the 'Apotheosis of Nelson', by Nicholas Legrand, both of which can be seen in the National Maritime Museum.

Treaty Pictures. The small group of Treaty or peace pictures forms an interesting addition to the main body of the Nelson pictures. They were published to celebrate the two short periods of peace during the course of the long Revolutionary and Napoleonic wars, the first the Treaty of Amiens (1802-3: nos. 64-66) and the second the brief period of peace following the Treaty of Paris (1814: nos. 69 and 70). In addition there are two similar pictures, dated 1806 (nos. 67 and 68), which probably refer to the ultimately unsuccessful negotiations between

Charles James Fox, Foreign Secretary of the Ministry of All the Talents, and Talleyrand, Napoleon's Foreign Minister, in the early months of that year. In each of these seven pictures Nelson is represented on a flag or as a bust, emphasising the extent to which he was widely perceived, and rightly so, as a major figure in the defeat of Napoleon. As such they clearly form an integral part of the popular iconography of Nelson, but it would be wrong to draw the conclusion that all Treaty pictures contained a reference to Nelson. On 2 May 1814, W.B. Walker produced a small picture, very similar to nos. 69 and 70, entitled 'Britannia's Triumph on the Restoration of Peace' but with no mention of Nelson. It may well be that there are other such pictures, but they must be rare.

THE PUBLISHERS OF THE PICTURES

The names of the nine firms which published the seventy listed glass pictures are set out in Table 1, three-quarters of the pictures being published by three firms – Hinton, Stampa and Walker. The dates of publication of these pictures, excluding the treaty pictures, are summarised in Table 2. Excluding the five pre-Trafalgar pictures (nos. 1-5) nearly half of these pictures were published within four months of the news of the battle reaching London in the early hours of 6 November 1805. The first three pictures (nos. 17-19), all by Hinton, were published on 21 November (see note to nos. 17 and 18).

Although none of the seventy glass pictures described in the catalogue are identical, there are a number of pairs, made up of a large and a small picture of essentially the same design, but often with small but distinct differences other than size. These thirteen pairs are summarised in Table 3. Not surprisingly the two pictures in a pair were always published by the same firm. In two instances (nos. 9 and 10, 46 and 47) both pictures were published on the same date, but in all the other pairs the smaller picture was published at a later date than the larger, suggesting perhaps that the larger picture had been a great success and the publisher decided that there would be a market for a smaller, no doubt cheaper, version.

There are eight glass pictures of which only a small version is known. It is possible that there was once a large version of each, particularly of nos. 4, 5, 27 and 31, which were published by Hinton, who published five other pictures in both large and small versions.

THE CATALOGUE

The catalogue is divided into four sections, corresponding with the four groups of pictures (Representational 1-36; Monumental 37-50; Allegorical 51-63; Treaty 64-70). The entry for each picture consists of a serial number, the title of the picture, the inscription below the title, including the name of the publisher and date of publication as set out in the picture, though in many instances a line of the inscription is too long to be reproduced legibly without a break. The style of type is followed as closely as possible. Notes about the pictures are appended when considered appropriate.

There is an illustration of each picture, except that where there is both a larger and a smaller version of the same picture (see page 21, Table 3), only one of each pair is usually illustrated to avoid duplication.

Tables 4-7 set out for each section of the catalogue the essential data for each picture and show, where applicable, the public galleries in which it can be seen.

There is no one single gallery in which most of these pictures can be seen. Of the pictures listed in this catalogue, twenty-two can be found only in private collections. There are twenty-five Nelson glass pictures in the National Maritime Museum, and three fine examples are in the museum's excellent Nelson Gallery. The remainder, though not on permanent display, can be seen on request. The Lily Lambert McCarthy Collection in the Royal Naval Museum, Portsmouth, contains twenty such pictures, most of which are on display. In the small but delightful Nelson Museum at Monmouth there are twenty-two glass pictures of Nelson: only a few are on display, but the remainder can be seen on request.

TABLE 1

PUBLISHERS OF NELSON GLASS PICTURES
with the number published by each and entries in London Post Office directories

Publisher	Number	Address on glass pictures	Entry in directory
I. [or J.] Hinton	29	44 Wells St., Oxford Street	[No entry found]
P. [or G.] Stampa	14	74 Leather Lane	1805: Barometer manufacturers, 25 Kirby Street [off Leather Lane]
W. B. Walker	10	Fox & Knot Court	[No entry found]
P. Barnaschina	6	73 Leather Lane	1805: Picture frame manufacturers, 4 Leather Lane
P. Patriarcha	4	Leather Lane	[No entry found]
P. Gally	3	7 Beauchamp Street, Leather Lane	[1805: no entry found]
P. & P. Gally	1	9 Turnmill Street	1815: Picture frame and looking glass maker, 9 Turnmill Street, Clerkenwell
J. Fairburn	2	146 The Minories	1805: Map, chart and print seller 146 The Minories
Unknown	2		
TOTAL	70		

NOTE: One picture, no. 64, was published jointly by P. Gally and P. Stampa.

TABLE 2

DATES OF PUBLICATION
of Nelson glass pictures (excluding the Treaty pictures,
of which the dates are those of the treaties)

Pre-Trafalgar		5
1805	November, last 2 weeks	5
	December	10
1806	January	8
	February	8
	March	11
	May	2
	June	4
	July	1
	September	1
	November-December	4
Unknown		4
TOTAL		63

TABLE 3

PAIRS OF PICTURES
with dates of publication

Nos.	Title	Publisher	Large	Small
7 & 8	Lord Nelson Commanding the Victory	Stampa	4 Dec. 1805	2 Jan. 1806
9 & 10	Admiral Lord Nelson fatally wounded by a musket shot	Walker	5 Dec. 1805	
11 & 12	Admiral Lord Nelson mortally wounded	Barnaschina	1 Feb. 1806	1 June 1806
14 & 15	Death of Lord Nelson	Stampa	4 Dec. 1805	2 Jan. 1806
37 & 38	Admiral Lord Nelson … gloriously fell fighting for his country	Stampa	14 Mar. 1806	2 June 1806
42 & 43	This Monumental Tribute of Success …	Hinton	6 Feb. 1806	1 Mar. 1806
44 & 45	Perpetuating the Memory of Lord Nelson etc.	Barnaschina	1 Feb. 1806	1 June 1806
46 & 47	Britannia lamenting the Death of Admiral Lord Nelson	Walker	5 Dec. 1805	
51 & 52	Ad. Nelson falling into the Arms of Victory	Hinton	12 Dec. 1805	1 Jan. 1806
57 & 58	The Death and Victory of AD. LD. NELSON	Hinton	12 Dec. 1805	1 Jan. 1805 [sic]
59 & 60	Britannia bringing her Dead Hero to Britannia's Shore	Hinton	6 Feb. 1806	1 Mar. 1806
61, 62 & 63	Neptune drawn by Sea Horses etc.	Stampa	(60 & 61) 14 Mar. 1806	(62) 2 June 1806
65 & 66	Victory Discovering to Neptune the Heros of the British Navy	Hinton	[?] 1803	29 June 1803

In each instance the smaller picture, the second of each pair, was published either on the same date as the larger one or later.

In three instances, the smaller picture consists of the centre portion of the larger, nos. 11 & 12; 44 & 45; 61, 62 & 63 (no. 63 consists of the main, central group of both no. 61 & no. 62).

The smaller picture of each pair is not illustrated except for nos. 38, 45, 63 and 66; except also for nos. 43 and 60, where the smaller picture is illustrated rather than the larger.

TABLE 4

REPRESENTATIONAL PICTURES

no.	Size	Orientation	Date	Publisher	Location and Reference		
					Nat. Marit. Mus.	R. Naval Mus.	Monmouth
1	Large	Vertical	1 Dec. 1800	Hinton			G632
2	Large	Horizontal	20 July 1801	Fairburn			
3	Large	Horizontal	20 July 1801	Fairburn			
4	Small	Horizontal	1 Sept. 1801	Hinton	GGG0521		
5	Small	Vertical	1 Aug. 1805	Hinton			
6	Large	Vertical	24 Dec. 1805	Hinton	GGG0531		
7	Large	Vertical	4 Dec.1805	Stampa		160	
8	Small	Vertical	2 Jan. 1806	Stampa			
9	Large	Vertical	5 Dec. 1805	Walker	GGG0507	145	G615
10	Small	Vertical	5 Dec. 1805	Walker			G637
11	Large	Horizontal	1 Feb. 1806	Barnaschina			
12	Small	Vertical	1 June 1806	Barnaschina			
13	Small	Vertical	[not visible]				
14	Large	Vertical	4 Dec. 1806	Stampa		159	
15	Small	Vertical	2 Jan. 1806	Stampa			
16	Small	Vertical	16 Dec. 1805	Patriarcha	GGG0498		
17	Large	Vertical	21 Nov 1805	Hinton	GGG0497		G616
18	Large	Vertical	21 Nov. 1805	Hinton			
19	Large	Vertical	21 Nov. 1805	Hinton			G634
20	Small	Vertical	16 Dec. 1805	Patriarcha			
21	Large	Horizontal	1 Jan. 1806	Hinton			
22	Large	Horizontal	14 March 1806	Stampa	GGG0520	152	
23	Large	Horizontal	24 Feb. 1806	Hinton	GGG0528		
24	Large	Horizontal	1 March 1806	Walker	GGG0526		G620
25	Large	Horizontal	15 March 1806	Hinton	GGG0529	151	
26	Large	Horizontal	[15 March 1806]	[Hinton]			
27	Small	Horizontal	1 July 1806	Hinton			
28	Large	Horizontal	? Sept. 1806	Barnaschina			G611
29	Large	Horizontal	1 Feb. 1806	Walker			G612
30	Large	Horizontal	1 Feb. 1806	Walker	GGG0503	150	
31	Small	Horizontal	[18]06	Hinton			
32	Large	Horizontal	11 Feb. 1806	Hinton			G622
33	Large	Horizontal	10 March 1806	Stampa	GGG0517		G624
34	Large	Horizontal	1 Nov. 1806	Barnaschina	GGG0518		G621
35	Large	Horizontal	18 May 1806	Hinton		149	G603
36	Large	Horizontal	18 May 1806	Hinton			

TABLE 5

MONUMENTAL PICTURES

no.	Size	Orientation	Date	Publisher	Location and Reference		
					Nat. Marit. Mus.	R. Naval Mus.	Monmouth
37	Large	Horizontal	14 March 1806	Stampa			G630
38	Small	Horizontal	2 June 1806	Stampa	GGG0512		
39	Large	Horizontal	20 Jan. 1806	Walker	GGG0509		
40	Large	Horizontal	20 Jan. 1806	Walker	GGG0527	156	G606
41	Large	Horizontal	11 March 1806	Patriarcha		147	
42	Large	Horizontal	6 Feb. 1806	Hinton		153	G607
43	Small	Horizontal	1 March 1806	Hinton	GGG0508		
44	Large	Horizontal	1 Feb. 1806	Barnaschina	GGG0499		
45	Small	Vertical	1 June 1806	Barnaschina	GGG0506		
46	Large	Vertical	5 Dec. 1805	Walker	GGG0502		
47	Small	Vertical	5 Dec. 1805	Walker		164	G636
48	Large	Horizontal	25 Nov. 1805	Gally			G609
49	Large	Horizontal	1 Dec. 1806	Stampa			G605
50	Small	Vertical	[not visible]				

TABLE 6

ALLEGORICAL PICTURES

no.	Size	Orientation	Date	Publisher	Location and Reference		
					Nat. Marit. Mus.	R. Naval Mus.	Monmouth
51	Large	Horizontal	12 Dec. 1805	Hinton	GGG0495		
52	Small	Horizontal	1 Jan. 1806	Hinton		163	
53	Large	Horizontal	25 Nov. 1805	Gally	GGG0530		
54	Large	Horizontal	11 March 1806	Patriarcha	GGG0551	148	
55	Large	Horizontal	20 Jan. 1806	Walker	GGG0493	162	G619a
56	Large	Horizontal	1 Dec. 1806	Stampa		161	G604
57	Large	Horizontal	12 Dec. 1805	Hinton	GGG0532		
58	Small	Horizontal	1 Jan. 1805 [sic]	Hinton		146	
59	Large	Horizontal	6 Feb. 1806	Hinton		155	G602
60	Small	Horizontal	1 March 1806	Hinton			
61	Large	Horizontal	14 March 1806	Stampa	GGG0504		
62	Large	Horizontal	14 March 1806	Stampa		157	
63	Small	Horizontal	2 June 1806	Stampa		154	

TABLE 7

TREATY PICTURES

no.	Size	Orientation	Date	Publisher	Location and Reference		
					Nat. Marit. Mus.	R. Naval Mus.	Monmouth
64	Large	Horizontal	16 Aug. 1802	Gally & Stampa			
65	Large	Horizontal	? 1803	Hinton			
66	Small	Horizontal	29 June 1803	Hinton			
67	Large	Horizontal	12 Aug. 1806	Hinton			
68	Large	Horizontal	12 Aug. 1806	Hinton			
69	Large	Horizontal	17 June 1814	P. & P. Gally		45	
70	Large	Horizontal	3 Sept. 1814	Hinton			G627

REPRESENTATIONAL PICTURES

No. 1 (large)

Right Honble HORATIO NELSON

Duke of Bronte in Naples, Baron Nelson, of the Nile, & of Burnham Thorpe, in the County of Norfolk, & K.B.
Rear Admiral of the Red, &c.

Published Dec, 1, 1800, by Hinton, N° 44, top of Well Street, Oxford Street, London.

NOTES. (i) This is the earliest of the Nelson glass pictures, the remainder being published after Trafalgar, except for (a) three pictures published in 1801 after the Battle of Copenhagen, 2 April 1801, namely, two pictures of the battle published on 20 July 1801, nos. 2 and 3, and a portrait published on 1 Sept. 1801, no. 4, and (b) a portrait published on 1 Aug. 1805, no. 5.

(ii) In terms of detail it is the glass picture giving the most accurate representation of Nelson. The gold braid at his wrist is accurate for his rank at that period of his career, Rear-Admiral. The caption is correct in stating that Nelson was a Rear-Admiral of the Red at the time of publication of this picture, but at the Nile (1 Aug. 1798) he was a Rear-Admiral of the Blue. Nelson was promoted to Rear-Admiral of the Red on 4 February 1799, 'jumping' the rank of Rear-Admiral of the White on account of his services at the Nile.

(iii) The two medals around his neck are for the Battle of Cape St. Vincent and for the Nile, the St. Vincent medal is probably the upper of the two. The decorations on his left breast are those of the Turkish Order of the Crescent, the Order of the Bath and the Neapolitan Order of Ferdinand and Merit. In his hat is the *chelengk*, presented to Nelson by the Sultan of Turkey.

(iv) The scabbard and hilt of the sword in Nelson's left hand is in the form of a crocodile, the pommel representing the crocodile's head. This sword was presented to Nelson after the Battle of the Nile by his captains in that action.

1

No. 2 (large)

Plate 1
A VIEW of ADMIRAL LORD NELSON's ATTACK upon the DANISH LINE before COPENHAGEN April 2nd 1801.

which consisted of 24 Ships of the Line and Floating Batteries laying moored: flanked & supported by the Crown Islands, on which were mounted 88 Guns, and also Batteries on the Shore. (See Plate 2)

Published 20th July 1801, by John Fairburn, 146, Minories, London.

NOTES TO NOS. 2 AND 3. (i) These two pictures, both rare, are the only known glass pictures celebrating the Battle of Copenhagen and the only known Nelson glass pictures published by Fairburn.

(ii) In a war entered into against old friends (with reluctance), the victory was not greeted with rejoicing of the same magnitude as that engendered by the news of the Battle of the Nile, or of Trafalgar. Nelson was created a viscount, but much to his annoyance the King forbade the issue of a victory medal (see above, no. 1, note iii), and the City of London did not mark this victory, as was their custom, with gifts to the victorious admirals and captains: see *Dispatches and Letters of Lord Nelson*, ed. H. Nicholas (1845), vol. iv, pp. 524-30; C. Oman, *Nelson* (1947), p. 496.

No. 3 (large)

Plate 2
A VIEW of ADMIRAL LORD NELSON's HEROIC VICTORY over the DANES before COPENHAGEN April 2nd 1801.

The British Squadron bore down consisting of 12 Ships of the Line and 17 Frigates, Sloops and Bombs,
when after a desparate Action of 4 hours, 17 of the Danish Ships were Sunk, Burnt or Taken,

Published 20th July, 1801, by John Fairburn, 146, Minories, London.

NOTES (cont.) (iii) The floating batteries referred to in the caption to no. 2 can be seen to the left of the centre line, about one third of the vertical height above the caption. The shore can be seen on the far right.

(iv) The red globe in no. 2 must represent the sun, red as seen through the smoke of the battle. The brown object apparently attached to the top of the sun is an artefact.

(v) The colouring of no. 3 suggests that the battle was fought at night. This was not the case, Nelson having been rowed ashore at about 2.0 p.m. to negotiate the cease fire. The dramatic colouring, as with the red sun in no. 2, presumably represents the effect of thick gunsmoke on the sunlight, possibly recording, at least in part, an eye-witness description of the scene.

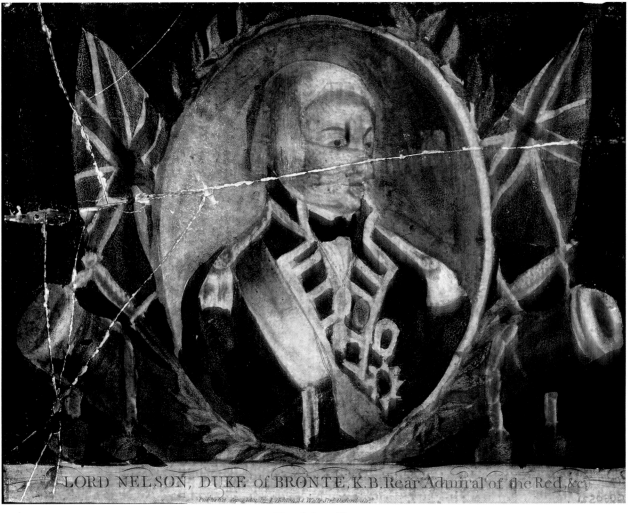

No. 4 (small)

LORD NELSON, DUKE of BRONTE, K.B. Rear Admiral of the Red etc.

Publish'd Sep 1, 1801 by I. Hinton 44 Wells Str^t, Oxford Str^t

© National Maritime Museum, London
(Negative no. EO268)

NOTES. (i) Published five months after the Battle of Copenhagen. Nelson's rank is incorrectly stated; he had been promoted to Vice-Admiral of the Blue on 1 January 1801.

(ii) A rare picture, of which the author has seen only this broken version.

No. 5 (small)

ADMIRAL NELSON.

Pub. Aug. 1. 1805. by I. Hinton 44 Wells Str.

NOTE. The only 1805 picture of Nelson published before Trafalgar.

No. 6 (large)

ADMIRAL LORD NELSON.

Published, Dec 24ᵗʰ 1805. by I. Hinton, 44, top of Wells Street, Oxford & Nᵒ. 10, Fox & Not Court, Cow Lane.

NOTE. This picture and nos. 7 and 8 are the only pictures of Nelson published after the news of Trafalgar reached London showing him before his fatal wound.

No. 7 (large)

LORD NELSON COMMANDING THE VICTORY.
Octr. 21. 1805.

London, Pub ^{d}. by P. Stampa, 74, Leather Lane, Holborn Dec. 4. 1805.
NOTE. See note to no. 6.

No. 8 (small)   (*not illustrated*)

LORD NELSON COMMANDING THE VICTORY.
Octr. 21. 1805

London, Pub^d. by P. Stampa, 74, Leather Lane, Holborn Jan. 2. 1806.
NOTE. A small version of no. 7; otherwise identical.

No. 9 (large)

*Admiral Ld Nelson mortally wounded by a Musket Ball, in the ever memorable Victory off
Trafalgar: on 21 Oct. 19 Sail of the Enemy struck their Colours, 1 blew up in the Action, 13 run away, &
4 of them were afterwards captured by Sir Richard Strachan, off Ferrol, 1 Novr. 1805.*

Pub^d. Decr 5, 1805, by W. B. Walker, Fork & Knot C^o, Snow Hill, London.

NOTE TO NOS. 9-16. The eight pictures are incorrect in that when struck over his left shoulder by a musket
ball Nelson fell not into the arms of an officer but on the deck. As Hardy rushed up Nelson said to him
'They have done for me at last, Hardy: my backbone is shot through.' Nelson was then picked up and
carried down to the cockpit, on the orlop deck. See also notes to nos. 17 and 18, and Appendix II.

No. 10 (small)

ADMIRAL LORD NELSON MORTALLY WOUNDED BY A MUSKET SHOT

London Pub^d Decr 5 1805, by W. B. Walker; Fork & Knot Co^t, Snow Hill.

NOTE. A small version of no. 9; otherwise identical except that (i) there is no gold medal around Nelson's neck, (ii) the caption is shorter.

No. 11 (large)

Admiral Lord Nelson mortally wounded by a Musket Ball in the moment of
                                        brilliant and decisive Victory over the combined
                    Fleets of France & Spain Octr. 21, 1805.

Pub^d. Feb 1 1806. Peter Barnaschina 73, Leather Lane, Holborn.

No. 12 (small)

Lord Nelson falling honorably in the service of his Country in the
Victory off Trafalgar Oct. 21. 1805.

Pub^d June 1 1806, by Barnaschina 73 Leather Lane Holborn.

NOTE. A small vertical version of the central group of figures in no. 11; otherwise identical except that (a) the ships etc. seen beyond the bulwark are slightly different, and (b) the caption is shorter. No. 12 was published four months after no. 11.

No. 13 (small)

DEATH *of* ADMIRAL LORD NELSON *Oct*. *21· 1805*

[Name and date of publisher not visible.]

No. 14 (large)

DEATH OF LORD NELSON,
Oct ʳ. 21. 1805.

London. Pubᵈ. by P. Stampa, 74, Leather lane, Holborn. Dec 4. 1805.

No. 15 (small)   (*not illustrated*)

DEATH OF LORD NELSON, *Oct ʳ. 21. 1805.*

London. Pubⁱ. by P. Stampa, 74, Leather Lane, Holborn. Jan 2. 1806.

NOTE. A small version of no. 14, identical save for details.

No. 16 (small)

The Ever-to-be Lament'd DEATH of LORD NELSON. Who was shot by a Musket Ball in the Brave & GLO RIOUS VICTORY, over the Combined Fleets of FRANCE & SPAIN, near Cape Trafalgar, Octr. 21. 1805

Pub^d. Dec 16, 1805 by Patriarcha, Leather Lane, London

No. 17 (large)

ADMIRAL LORD NELSON, giving his last ORDERS to CAP. HARDY,
of the Victory after he was mortally wounded, Oct. 21. 1805.

Pub. Nov. 21.1805. by I. Hinton, 44 Well Sᵗ. Oxford Sᵗ. London.

NOTE. See notes overleaf to nos. 17 and 18.

No. 18 (large)

ADMIRAL LORD NELSON, giving his last ORDERS to CAP. HARDY
of the Victory after he was mortally Wounded, Oct. 21.1805.

Pub. Nov. 21.1805. by I. Hinton, 44 Well S'. Oxford S'. London.

NOTES TO NOS. 17 and 18. (i) The two pictures are the same except that no. 18 has the addition of two seamen serving the gun and two marines on the poop, each with a musket firing upwards. It is of interest that both pictures were published on the same day.

(ii) In fact Nelson gave his last orders to Hardy ('Anchor, Hardy, anchor') not while he was still on the quarterdeck but as he lay dying in the cockpit of the *Victory*.

(iii) Collingwood's dispatch with news of the battle arrived in London in the early hours of 5 November, and was published as a special Gazette in *The Times* on 7 November, so that it could well have been widely known by 21 November that 'his Lordship received a musket ball in the L. Breast', leading to his death some three hours later. No mention was made in the dispatch of the fact that the musket ball was fired from the maintop of the *Redoutable*, and that shortly afterwards the man firing the shot was himself killed by a musket ball fired by a marine on the deck of the *Victory*. It may well be that the two figures with muskets, on the poop, aiming above the horizontal, represent marines firing at the maintop of the ship alongside, and that this further detail relating to Nelson's death had been learnt by word of mouth from the crew of the *Pickle*, the schooner that carried Collingwood's dispatch to England.

(iv) Only one decoration is shown on Nelson's coat. On the morning of the battle he wore his usual Vice-Admiral's undress coat, with four decorations on the left breast, the three detailed above in note (iii) to no. 1 and the Maltese Cross of the Order of St. Joachim.

(v) In the background a ship is shown blowing up. This must represent the French ship *Achille*, which exploded after surrendering, an episode mentioned by Collingwood in his dispatch, though in fact the explosion occurred several hours after Nelson was wounded.

(vi) Note the figures on the poop of the French ship, one of whom is pulling down the ensign, while two others are raising their arms in surrender.

ADMIRAL LORD NELSON, giving his last ORDERS to CAP. HARDY, of the Victory, after he was mortally Wounded, Oct. 21, 1805.

18

Figure A

THE DEATH OF NELSON

Reproduced from the painting by Arthur William Devis in the Nelson Gallery of the National Maritime Museum. There is another version of the painting, possibly a preliminary study, in the cockpit of H.M.S. *Victory*.

© National Maritime Museum
(Negative no. BHC2894)

The kneeling figure on Nelson's left, feeling his pulse, is William Beatty, surgeon to the *Victory*. On Beatty's right is Chevalier, Nelson's steward, and beyond him Walter Burke, the purser. Bending over this group is the tall figure of Thomas Hardy, Captain of the *Victory*. On Nelson's right, rubbing his chest, is the Revd. Alexander Scott, chaplain to the *Victory*.

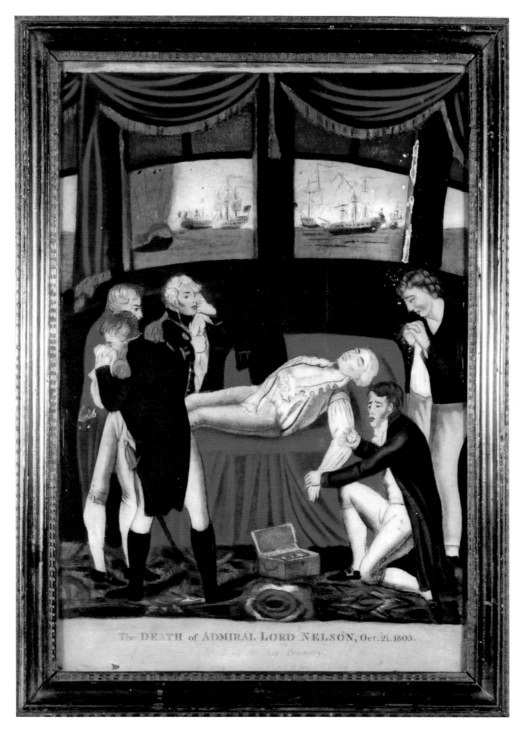

No. 19 (large)

The DEATH of ADMIRAL LORD NELSON, Oct. 21 1805.
He Died for his Country.

Pub. Nov 21. 1805. I. Hinton. Well Sᵗ. Oxford Sᵗ. London

NOTE. In all respects a highly inaccurate, romanticised version of the actual scene; compare with
the scene as painted by Devis, and reproduced opposite.

No. 20 (small)

ADMIRAL LORD COLLINGWOOD receiving the French and Spanish
ADMIRALS SWORDS on board the R. Sovereign after the GLORIOUS VICTORY

Pub Dec. 16 1805 by P. Patriarcha Leather Lane. London

NOTES. (i) After the Spanish ship the *Santa Ana* had surrendered to the *Royal Sovereign* Collingwood sent Blackwood (captain of the frigate *Euryalus*) 'to go on board the *Santa Ana*, and bring the Spanish Admiral to me; he returned soon after with her captain who delivered to me the Spanish Admiral's sword, and informed me that the Vice-Admiral De Alava was so dangerously wounded that he was near expiring.' [From Collingwood's journal, the excerpt kindly supplied by Capt. C.H.H. Owen, R.N. (retd.).] It may well be this scene that is represented in this picture.

(ii) Although Nelson is neither shown nor mentioned in this picture, it is included as integrally related to Nelson.

(iii) Collingwood is incorrectly given the title Admiral Lord Collingwood. At the time of the battle he was a Vice Admiral and a baronet. He was created a baron shortly after the battle, but never obtained the rank of full Admiral.

No. 21 (large)

The Situation of the VICTORY, & the rest of the FLEET after the engagement
with the Combined Fleets of FRANCE & SPAIN,
on the 21, Oct, 1805 under the command of Adm^l. COLLINGWOOD.

Pub. Jan 1. 1806, by I. Hinton 44 Well S^t. & 10 Fox & Not Court Cow Lane.

NOTES. (i) The *Victory* is correctly shown having lost her mizzen mast, and with damage to her main and foremast.

(ii) The ship exploding must represent the destruction of the French ship the *Achille*, which exploded after being burnt to the waterline.

(iii) In illustrating the situation of the British fleet 'after the engagement with the combined fleets of France and Spain' the caption is correct in stating that it was under the command of Collingwood, who assumed command after the death of Nelson.

(iv) Following the battle Collingwood never returned to England but continued in command of the fleet in the Mediterranean until his death, at sea off Minorca, 7 March 1810. He lies buried in the crypt of St. Paul's, beside Nelson.

No. 22 (large)

Representation of the BODY of the Late Illustrious ADMIRAL LORD NELSON *laying in STATE in the* Painted Hall *at* Greenwich Hospital.

London. Published March 14ᵗʰ, 1806.   *by Stampa & Son 74 Leather Lane*

Figure B

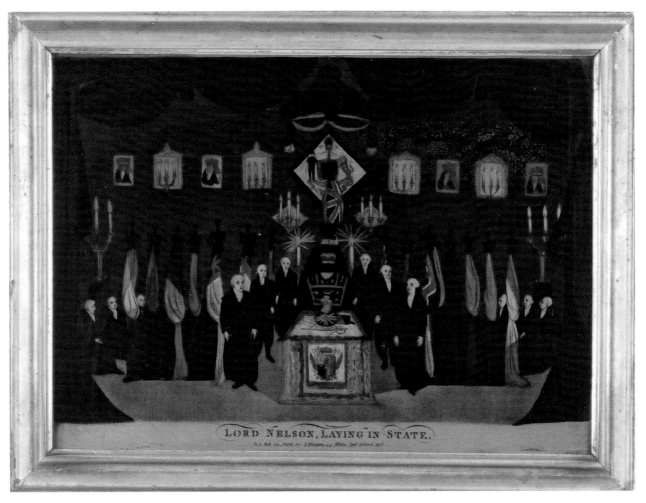

No. 23 (large)

LORD NELSON, LAYING IN STATE.

Pub. Feb. 24. 1806, by I. Hinton, 44, Wells Str^t. Oxford Str^t.

NOTE. Lord Nelson's body lay in state in the Painted Hall, Greenwich, on 5, 6 and 7 January; in those three days more than 30,000 people passed through the hall to view the coffin. By comparison with the Pugin print (Figure B, opposite), it is clear that the glass pictures, nos. 22 and 23, give a remarkably accurate representation of the scene. There is a fascinating, detailed account of all the stages of Nelson's funeral in Archibald Duncan's *Life of the Late Most Noble Lord, Horatio Nelson* (London and Liverpool, 1806). It states that on the first two days there were two attendants on each side of the coffin but on the third there were three; the pall was removed, and Nelson's viscount's coronet was removed from the head to the foot of the coffin; that indicates that the glass pictures record the scene on the third day.

No. 24 (large)

*A Correct Representation of the Funeral Barge which conveyed the
Body of the late Lord Nelson from Greenwich to Whitehall, Jany. 8th. 1806.*

London Published March 1, 1806, by W. B. Walker, Fox & Knot Co. Cow Lane.

Figure C

No. 25 (large)

A Correct Representation of the Funeral Barge which conveyed the
Body of the late Lord Nelson from Greenwich to Whitehall, Jan. 8ᵗʰ. 1806.

Pub. March 15, 1806, by I. Hinton, 44, Wells Strᵗ. Oxford Strᵗ.

NOTE TO NOS. 24-28. (i) In broad terms the five glass pictures give a recognisable representation of Nelson's funeral barge which, together with part of the procession on the river, is more accurately shown in Pugin's print (Figure C, opposite). The print shows only one flag on the funeral barge, the Union Jack at the bow, but each of the glass pictures shows three flags, the Royal Standard at the bow, Nelson's arms above his coffin and at the stern the Union Jack in the three published or assumed to be published by Hinton (nos. 25-27) and the White Ensign in the other two.

(ii) The print shows the barge being rowed upstream past Greenwich Hospital and Greenwich church on the south (or right) bank of the river.

(iii) The background to no. 25 is presumably a crude representation of Greenwich Hospital, with (correctly) the barge being rowed upstream. If, as is probably the case, the indeterminate row of houses forming the background to no. 24 is meant to represent the Greenwich shore, the barge is being rowed downstream.

(iv) For the bow and stern of the barge as shown in no. 24, see note to no. 28.

No. 26 (large)

A Correct Representation of the Funeral Barge which conveyed the
Body of the late Lord Nelson from Greenwich to Whitehall, Jan. 8ᵗʰ. 1806.

NOTES. (i) The name of the publisher and date of publication are not visible, but as this picture is similar in all important respects, including the caption, to no. 25, it seems reasonable to assume that it was published by Hinton.

(ii) Clearly copies of the same print were used for nos. 25 and 26, which differ only, but markedly, in the background. It seems that in no. 25 the unskilled artist employed to colour the back of the picture substituted a simpler background, omitting the detail shown in that of no. 26.

No. 27 (small)

The Funeral Barge which conveyed the Body of the late Lord Nelson
from Greenwich to Whitehall. Jan. 8ᵗʰ 1806

Pubᵈ July 1 1806   *by J. Hinton. Well Sᵗ. Oxford Sᵗ.*

NOTE. Essentially a smaller version of nos. 25 and 26, with no space to show the accompanying vessels, it differs in two important respects, (a) there are only four, not five, pairs of oarsmen (b) the barge is proceeding downstream and the wind is blowing from the east.

No. 28 (large)

A Correct Representation of the Funeral Barge which conveyed the
Body of the late Lord Nelson from Greenwich to Whitehall, Jan. 8ᵗʰ. 1806.

London. Pubᵈ. Septʳ 1806, by P. Barnaschina, 32 Baldwin Gardens.

NOTE. Nelson's funeral barge did not have a figurehead of an angel holding out a wreath, nor was the stern constructed to resemble the stern of a ship of the line, as shown in this picture and in no. 24. It seems that the artist transferred these features from those of the funeral car (see nos. 29-34).

No. 29 (large)

A Correct Representation of the Funeral Car which conveyed the
Body of Lord Nelson from the Admiralty to S[t]. Pauls, Jan[y]. 9th. 1806.

London, Published Feb[y]. 1. 1806. by W. B. Walker, 4, Fox & Knot Court, Cow Lane.

Figure D

Pugin's print showing Nelson's coffin, in a magnificent funeral car, arriving at St. Paul's Cathedral at the head of the procession from the Admiralty. Although varying in detail, the six pictures nos. 29-34 of the funeral car are essentially correct. It is sad that no. 31 does not show all six horses.

No. 30 (large)

A Correct Representation of the Funeral Car which conveyed the
Body of Lord Nelson from the Admiralty to St Pauls, Jany. 9th. 1806.

London. Published Feby. 1 1806 by W. B. Walker & Son, 4, Fox & Knot Court^y. Cow Lane.

NOTE. Nos. 29 and 30 are of interest as they were published on the same date, 1 Feb. 1806, and by the same firm, yet they differ in important respects, notably the shape of the ensign and the angle of the figure at the front of the funeral car. These differences indicate that the pictures were made from different prints, rather than representing changes made after the print had been applied to the glass. See note to no. 40.

No. 31 (small)
LORD NELSON's FUNERAL CAR

[18]06   by I. Hinton 44 Well St

NOTE. Date of publication not legible, except for . . 06

No. 32 (large)
LORD NELSON'S FUNERAL CAR.

Pub. Feb. 17. 1806. by J. Hinton, 44, Wells S^t. London.

31

32

No. 33 (large)

London. Publish'd March 10, 1806, by THE MAGNIFICENT FUNERAL CAR. *Stampa & Son. 74, Leather lane*
which was Built *for the* purpose *of* conveying *the* Remains *of* Vice-Admiral Lord
Nelson, *to* St Paul's Cathedral, *for* Interment, *on Thursd^y Jan. 9. 1806.*

No. 34 (large)

A Correct Representation of the Funeral Car now Exhibiting in the Painted Chamber Greenwich Hospital.

London, Pub, Nov 1, 1806, by P. Barnaschina, 32 Baldwins Gardens.

No. 35 (large)

This picture is divided into two portions vertically by a mast or spar.

The Death of A^D. L^D. NELSON

The Monument of A^D. L^D. NELSON
who Died for his Country.

Pub. May 18. 1806. by I. Hinton 44, Wells Str^t.

NOTE. The left half of this picture is similar in most respects to no. 19 and the right half to nos. 42 and 43, but each half does not just represent a reproduction of the individual prints. Thus, in the left half, two of the standing figures are omitted and in the right half the background to the mourning sailor is simplified, and with her left arm Britannia is comforting a weeping boy, not holding a shield. Further, the proportions of each half differ from those in the single pictures. This is particularly noticeable in the right half, where in no. 42 the vertical axis is shorter than the horizontal, whereas the opposite is the case in the double picture. It is clear that no. 35 required the production of a new print. All the pictures were published by Hinton, no. 19 on 21 November 1805 and no. 42 on 6 February 1806.

No. 36 (large)

This picture is divided into two portions, vertically, by a mast or spar.

A^D. L^D. NELSON   A^D. L^D. NELSON
giving his last orders to Capt.Hardy.

Pub May 18, 1806. by I. Hinton 44 Wells Str^t.

NOTE. The right half of this picture is in essentials similar to nos. 17 and 18, except for the omission of the figure of the wounded officer lying on the deck. No picture has been found closely resembling the left half of this picture, which may, perhaps, have been drawn to make up a double picture. That seems unlikely, however, since nos. 35 and 36 were both published by Hinton on the same day, 18 May 1806, and since both halves of no. 35 and the right half of no. 36 were closely based on prints previously published by Hinton. It therefore seems probable either that the left half was based on an as yet undiscovered glass picture, or that it is based on no. 6, a picture published by Hinton on 24 December 1805. In no. 6 Nelson has in his left hand a trumpet, not a sword, and he is not accompanied by a midshipman; but the stance of Nelson himself, the angle of his hat, his decorations etc. are so similar that it may well be that no. 6 was in fact the basis of the left half of no. 36.

MONUMENTAL PICTURES

No. 37 (large)

A Monumental Tribute *of RESPECT, to the* Memory *of* ADMIRAL LORD NELSON, *who in the* Moment *of* VICTORY,
Gloriously fell, *Fighting for* his COUNTRY

London Published March 14ᵗʰ. 1806   *by Stampa & Son, 74, Leather Lane.*

> NOTE. Most of the glass pictures, especially the Monumental pictures, are incorrect in the way that they show the Union Jack and the Union flag forming one quarter of the White Ensign. Following the Union with Ireland, in 1801, the red diagonal cross of St. Patrick was enclosed within the white diagonal cross of St. Andrew. Whereas in a few pictures (e.g. no. 17) the flag is correctly shown, it is clear that most of the artists who designed the pictures were confused on the point.

No. 38 (small)

ADMIRAL LORD NELSON, who Gloriously fell fighting for his COUNTRY

London Published June 2ᵈ. 1806. by Stampa & Son, 74 Leather Lane.

NOTES. (i) A simplified version of no. 37. Note that (a) the monument is topped by a plain black pyramid, rather than a pyramidal structure decorated with a picture of Britannia with a shield and lion etc. (b) the decoration behind the portrait of Nelson is different (c) the plinth has no inscription (d) there is no building in the background.

(ii) The inscription is briefer and the date of publication later than that of no. 37.

No. 39 (large)

A Monumental Tribute of Respect to the Memory of Admiral Lord Nelson
            who in the moment of Victory gloriously fell fighting for his country on the
21 Oct'. 1805.

Pub^d Jan^r. 20. 1806, by W. B. Walker, Fox & Knot Co^1., Snow Hill, London.

No. 40 (large)

A Monumental Tribute of Respect to the Memory of Admiral Lord Nelson
who in the moment of Victory gloriously fell fighting for his Country on the
21 Oct'. 1805.

Pub^d. Jan. 20. 1806, by W. B. Walker, Fox & Knot Co'., Snow Hill, London.

NOTE. This picture is quite different from no. 39, but the inscription is precisely the same, and it was published on the same date by the same publisher. See note to no. 30: in that instance the differences between the pictures were less marked.

No. 41 (large)

Britania Weeping for the Loss of Her Much Lamented HERO ADMIRAL NELSON,
         & an Officer holding the PALM of MERIT which he so
GLORIOUSLY gained in Defence of his Country, he fell in the memorable Battle of
         Trafalgar, in the Moment of VICTORY, having been in
121 different engagements, both by SEA & LAND and CONQUERED in above 100,
        of them, To the Glory of the BRITISH NATION.

London Pub. March 11, 1806, by P. Patriarcha, Leather Lane.

No. 42 (large)   *(not illustrated)*

This MONUMENTAL TRIBUTE of Respect to the Memory of A^d. L^d. NELSON,
         who in the moment of Victory gloriously fell fighting
for his Country is Dedicated to the Navy of Great Britain.

Pub. Feb 6 1806, by I Hinton, 44 Wells St^t., Oxford St^t., London.

No. 43 (small)

This MONUMENTAL TRIBUTE of Respect to the Memory of A^d. I^d. NELSON,

who in the moment of Victory gloriously fell fighting

for his country is Dedicated to the Navy of Great Britain.

Published March 1. 1806. by I. Hinton, N°. 44 top of Wells Street, Oxford Street, London.

NOTES. (i) In all essentials a small version of no. 42, except that on either side, instead of plain blue edging, there is a narrow strip of sea and sky, with the stern of the ships.

(ii) The spacing of the caption and the date of publication differs from no. 42.

No. 44 (large)

A Tribute of Gratitude to British Valour and Intrepidity commemorating
the glorious services of Admiral Lord Nelson who
fell gloriously fighting for his Country Octr 21 1805.

Pub^d Feby 1. 1806 by Peter Barnaschina, 73 Leather Lane, Holborn

No. 45 (small)

A Monumental Design to perpetuate the Memory of Lord Nelson who
Fell Oct.ʳ 21 1805

Pub. June 1. 1806, by P. Barnaschina, 73 Leather Lane Holborn.

NOTE. This picture is in all essentials the same as the centre portion of no. 44, the only differences being (a) flags on either side of the two weeping angels, replacing the figures of Britannia and a sailor (b) the inclusion of the draping curtains at the top (c) the inclusion of the banner with his name above his bust and (d) the caption is much shorter. It was published four months after no. 44; both were published by Barnaschina.

No. 46 (large)

*Brittannia lamenting the death of **Admiral Lord Nelson**, who after a series of transcendant and heroic Virtues, fell gloriously in his 121ˢᵗ. Engagement in the Moment of a Brilliant & Decisive Victory, obtained over the Combined Fleets of France & Spain on the 21ˢᵗ. Octʳ. 1805.*

Pub. Dec 5 1805. W. B. Walker. Fox & Knot Coᵗ., Snow Hill, London.

NOTES. (i) There can be no doubt that this picture commemorates Nelson's victories and his death at Trafalgar, but it is of interest that the three wreaths commemorate the battles of Cape St. Vincent, at which Nelson was not in command of the fleet, the Nile and Copenhagen. But neither the picture nor the caption names Trafalgar, it presumably being assumed, no doubt correctly in 1806, that '21ˢᵗ. Octʳ. 1805' referred to the Battle of Trafalgar.

(ii) It is tempting to speculate that the right-hand part of the picture, the plinth with the wreaths and Nelson's picture, was originally drawn shortly after the Battle of Copenhagen and was later added to and used as a print to make a glass picture to commemorate Nelson's death.

No. 47 (small)   *(not illustrated)*

BRITTANNIA LAMENTING THE DEATH OF ADMIRAL LORD NELSON.

London. Pub^d. Decr 5. 1805 by W. B. Walker. Fox & Knot Co^t. Snow Hill.

NOTE. The same as no. 46 except for (a) size (b) caption (c) the wreath recording the Battle of the Nile is to the left of that recording the Battle of Copenhagen.

No. 48 (large)

Fame and Britannia Crown'd with Laurels - the BUST of the glorious
                         & VICTORIOUS HERO NELSON for the distinguish'd & Interesting
Service, which he has perform'd for the Benefit of his Country – This
                         NOBLE VETERAN having been in more than 121 different engagements by
SEA & LAND and succeeded in being VICTORIOUS in more than
                         100 of them – And History is Entering his NAME to Immortality.

London. Published by P. Gally, Novr. 25, 1805. No 7 Beauchamp Street, Leather Lane. Holborn.

NOTE. Some examples of this picture have a black triangle behind the bust of Nelson (as in no. 40), but are in all other respects identical with this picture.

No. 49 (large)

A Monumental Tribute of Respect to the Memory of Admiral Lord Nelson,

Born Septr. 26. 1758. Died October 21, 1805.

Publish'd Decr 1st 1806 by P. Stampa & Son. 74 Leather Lane. London.

NOTE. The picture on the panel in the centre is similar to no. 21.

No. 50 (small)

BRITANNIA LAMENTING *the* DEATH *of* L^D NELSON

[Name and date of publisher not visible.]

ALLEGORICAL
PICTURES

No. 51 (large)

ADMIRAL NELSON Falling into the Arms of VICTORY
The Rt. Honble. Vice Admiral Lord Viscount NELSON, Duke of BRONTE,
who was mortally WOUNDED by a MUSKET SHOT in the left Breast in the Action of the 21. Oct. 1805,
off Cape TRAFALGAR, with the Combined Fleets of FRANCE & SPAIN,
when 19 Sail of the LINE was taken, Sunk, or Destroyed, to the GLORY of the BRITISH SAILORS.

Pub. Dec. 12, 1805, by I. Hinton 44 Wells S^t., and No 10 Fox & Not Court, Cow Lane, London.

NOTE. The words on the scroll borne by the cherub are 'Victory fifteen sail has already struck'.

No. 52 (small)   *(not illustrated)*

AD. NELSON falling into the Arms of VICTORY.
A^d. L^d. Nelson fell in the Arms of Victory by a Wound in the left Breast,

Oct. 21, 1805. when 19 ships of the Combin'd
Fleets of France & Spain were taken Sunk or Destroy'd.

Pub. Jan.1. 1806, by I. Hinton 44, Wells S^t. & Oxford S^t., & No 10. Fox & Not Court, Cow Lane.

NOTE. Apart from the size and date of publication, the same as no. 51, except that (a) the cherub bearing a scroll is omitted, presumably on grounds of size, (b) the caption is shorter.

No. 53 (large)

The Noble Admiral LORD NELSON fell in the Arms of VICTORY by the wound in his left BREAST
from a Musket shot in the memorable
Battle on the 21st of Oct^{br}. 1805 at CAPE TRAFALGAR off CADIZ on board his MAJESTY's SHIP
the Victory, whilst engaging the SPANISH & FRENCH
FLEETS where 19 Ships of the ENEMYS LINE struck their Colours to the BRITISH FLAG, to the
Glory of the English Navy.

London. Published by P. Gally, Novr. 25 1805. No 7 Beauchamp Street, Leather Lane, Holborn.

NOTES. (i) On the stern of the sinking ship is its name, *S. Trinidada*, clearly representing the Spanish ship, *Santissima Trinidada* (140 guns), one of the largest vessels afloat. Severely damaged by the *Neptune* (98 guns), she surrendered to the *Prince* (98 guns), and then sank in the gale following the battle, not during the battle as illustrated here.

(ii) Across the stern of the second ship, flying the Red Ensign, is the name *Royal Sovereign*, in reverse, with the letters back to front. This suggests that, unlike the name *S. Trinidada*, which is clearly part of the initial print, this name was added by whoever painted the back of the glass, not realising that his addition would read back to front when viewed from the front: this interpretation is supported by the finding that in other copies of this print there is no name on the stern of this vessel. The *Royal Sovereign* was the flag ship of Vice-Admiral Sir Cuthbert Collingwood, second-in-command to Lord Nelson.

(iii) Concerning the flag, see no. 37, note.

No. 54 (large)

The Noble Admiral LORD NELSON, falling in the Arms of Victory, by a Mortal wound rec^d.

from a Musket ball in the left BREAST in the

memorable Battle of the 21. of Octr. 1805, at Cape Trafalgar, on board the Ship Victory –

his Brave Captn. Hardy telling his LORDSHIP

that 15 French & Spanish Ships had struck there Colours, – And in all, 19 of the Combin'd Fleets

struck to our Brave Tars.

London. Pub. March 11, 1806, by P. Patriarcha, Leather Lane.

NOTES. (i) Across the stern of the sinking vessel is the name *S. Trinidada*. See no. 53, note (i).

(ii) The distraught boy in the background, wringing his hands, is presumably a young mid-shipman.

(iii) Capt. Hardy informed Nelson about the number of the enemy fleet striking 'to our Brave Tars' not when Nelson fell on the quarterdeck but some time later when he visited him, shortly before his death, in the cockpit.

No. 55 (large)

Admiral Lord Nelson the Hero of the Nile, of the Battle of Copenhagen, falling

into the Arms of Victory in the ever-memorable

Engagement with the combined Fleets of France and Spain off Trafalgar, on the 21 Octr. 1805.

Pub^d. Jan 20, 1806, by W. B. Walker, Fox & Knot Co^t. Snow Hill, London.

NOTE. Across the stern of the sinking ship are the words *SANC^T. TRINIDADA.* See no. 53, note (i).

No. 56 (large)

The Noble Adm^i. L^d. Nelson, Mortally wounded by a Musket Ball, in the moment of brilliant and decisive Victory, over the Combined Fleets of France and Spain. October 21st. 1805.

Publish'd Decr. 1st. 1806 by P. Stampa & Son, 74, Leather Lane, London.

NOTE. One of the most delightful of the allegorical pictures. Nelson, his left hand held by Victory, is collapsing into the arms of Neptune. The eye, in the sky above, with radiating beams, presumably represents the Almighty.

No. 57 (large)

The DEATH & VICTORY of LORD NELSON

Neptune from his lowest bed
Mourns his darling Hero dead,
And Britain with a Mother's grief
Mourns her Slain Victorious Chief.

Bid Genius, bid in Hist'ry's page
His fame descend to ev'ry age,
While stor'd urns & trophies tell
How Nelson fought how Nelson fell.

Pub. Dec. 12. 1805. by I. Hinton. 44. Well S^t. & N°. 10, Fox & Not Court, Cow Lane, London.

No. 58 (small)   (not illustrated)

The DEATH & VICTORY of A^D. L^D. NELSON.

Bid genius, Bid History's page,   *While stor'd Urns & Trophies tell,*
His fame descend to ev'ry age.   *How Nelson fought, how Nelson fell.*

Pub. Jan 1, 1805. by I. Hinton, 44 Wells S^t. Oxford S^t., & No 10 Fox & Not Court, Cow Lane.

NOTES. (i) In all respects a smaller version of no. 57, except that the cupid in the top, right corner is omitted and in the inscription, which is different, there is room only for the second verse of the epic poem.

(ii) Whoever wrote the caption forgot that 1 January marks a New Year!

No. 59 (large)   (not illustrated)

BRITANNIA bringing her DEAD HERO
to BRITANNIA'S SHORE.

But hark the Cannon's sound the gen'ral tear   *That Ship which still his conquering Standard bore*
Proclains the Hero of Trafalgar near,   *Brought her dead Hero to Britannia's Shore.*

Pub. Feb 6. 1806. by I. Hinton, 44, Well S^t. Oxford S^t. London

NOTES. (i) Nelson reclines against the ample figure of Britannia, the two seated in an upholstered carriage, drawn by two white sea horses and fitted with a paddle wheel. A lion swims alongside the carriage, holding aloft a White Ensign, incorrectly drawn. An angel flies across the sky, bearing a banner, partly obscured by the ensign, reading 'ENGLAND … MAN WILL DO HIS DUTY'.

(ii) In the background there are several ships, including one blowing up, presumably the *Achille* (see note to no. 18).

No. 60 (small)

BRITANNIA bringing her DEAD HERO to BRITANNIA'S SHORE.

Pub. March 1. 1806, by I. Hinton, 44, Wells St^r. Oxford St London

NOTE. In all respects a small version of no. 59, except that the banner reads
'A^d. NELSON & EN…RY MAN TO DO HIS DUTY' and the inscription omits the verses.

No. 61 (large)

NEPTUNE drawn by Sea Horses, and preceded by TRITONS, bearing Emblematic Devices, *Supporting his Favourite Son* ADMIRAL LORD NELSON, *in his Last Moments.*

London, Published March 14, 1806   *by Stampa & Sons, 74 Leather Lane.*

NOTES. (i) Two of the Tritons carry flags, one inscribed 'Battle off the Nile', the other 'Battle off Copenhagen', while a third Triton holds aloft a model of a ship of the line, named *VICTORY* across its stern.

(ii) A mermaid in the sea holds out a white flag, on which are named six vessels captured or sunk in the battle of Trafalgar, four Spanish and two French, including the *Santissima Trinidada*, the largest vessel in the action, and the French ship, *Redoubtable* [sic], from which was fired the shot which mortally wounded Nelson.

(iii) It is tempting to speculate that this picture, published within a few weeks of the preceding two attractive pictures no. 59 & no. 60 by Hinton, and the succeeding two, represent the response of Stampa, in an effort to obtain his share of a profitable line developed by his rival.

No. 62 (large)   *(not illustrated)*

NEPTUNE drawn by Sea Horses, *and preceded by TRITONS, bearing* Emblematic Devices, *Supporting his favourite Son* ADMIRAL LORD NELSON *in his last moments.*

London, Published March 14, 1806   *by Stampa & Son, 74 Leather Lane*

NOTE. The picture is in all respects the same as no. 61, except that the Triton holding aloft a replica of the *Victory* is replaced by a castle, standing on a sea wall.

No. 63 (small)

NEPTUNE *f*upporting his favorite Son ADMIRAL LORD NELSON, in his last Moments.

London Published June 2, 1806, by Stampa & Son, 74, Leather Lane.

NOTES. (i) The picture consists of the central group from nos. 61 and 62, but without (a) the Tritons in the water (b) the female figure holding the sheet listing captured vessels (c) the cherubs in the sky above Nelson. In addition, there are no paddles on the wheels of Neptune's horse-drawn barge.

(ii) It is tempting to postulate that the two pictures published by Stampa in March 1806 were in such demand that in June he published this smaller and doubtless cheaper version.

TREATY PICTURES

No. 64 (large)

BRITANNIA, ʃupporting the PROTECTORS of PEACE & LIBERTY.

Publish'd Aug 16 1802. By   *P Gally 7 Beauchamp St', Brooks Market & G. Stampa,*
74 Leather Lane, Holborn.

NOTES. (i) Together with nos. 65 and 66 this picture celebrates the Treaty of Amiens, March 1802 –
May 1803.

(ii) The banner above the child's head reads 'PEACE LIBERTY and CONCORD'. The bust in Britannia's right
hand is engraved 'George III' and that in her left arm 'Nelson'.

(iii) See no. 69 note (i).

No. 65 (large)
VICTORY
Discovering to Neptune the Heros of the British Navy.

Arise British Heroes smiling rise,
Rous'd by the Martial Voice of Fame,

Her trump shall rend the echoing skies,
With Nelson, Duncan, & Vincent's Name.

[?] *1803, by I Hinton 44 Wells St. London*

NOTES. (i) The Admirals depicted and named on the Naval Pillar are: top row, Nelson, Duncan; middle row, Keith, St Vincent; bottom row, Sidney Smith, Cornwallis. Lord Duncan commanded the fleet which defeated the Dutch at the Battle of Camperdown, October 1797. Lord Keith commanded the fleet in the North Sea during the Trafalgar campaign. Lord St. Vincent, a formidable disciplinarian, commanded the fleet at the Battle of Cape St. Vincent, February 1797. Sir Sidney Smith defended Acre in 1799, frustrating Napoleon's attempt to return from Egypt to France by land. Sir William Cornwallis commanded the Western fleet blockading Brest during the Trafalgar campaign.

(ii) The inscription on the base of the pillar reads
ERECTED IN HONOUR OF
THE BRITISH NAVAL OFFICERS
AND SEAMEN.

No. 66 (small)

VICTORY
Discovering to Neptune the Heros of the British Navy.

Pub. June 29, 1803, by I. Hinton 44 Wells Str^t. Oxford Str^t. London.

NOTES. (i) A small version of no. 65, without any names or lettering on the Naval Pillar.

(ii) On 14 March 1803 Hinton published a pair of small glass pictures related to the Treaty of Amiens. The first, entitled 'BRITANNIA'S Glory Fame proclaiming PEACE' shows Britannia in a chariot drawn by sea horses, similar to that in nos. 59-63, holding aloft two banners, one decorated with a portrait of George III, the other that of (probably) an admiral, but there is nothing indicating that it is actually Nelson. The second, with no naval connections or symbols, is entitled 'NEPTUNE introducing the Four Quarters of the World to COMMERCE'. (See no. 68, note.)

No. 67 (large)
BRITANNIA'S GLORY.

Chear up Britannia, dissipate all Fears,   Let home bred concord Britain's Peace complete,
Peace on thy Borders from each coast appears,   Let discord cease, malicious strife retreat.

Pub. Augt. 12 1806 I. Hinton, 44, Wells Str^t. Oxford Str^t. London

NOTES. (i) See note to no. 68.
(ii) The lettering on the flag reads:

*The HERO
of
TRAFALGAR*

No. 68 (large)
VICTORY *conducting* PLENTY
to the Temple of Peace

Commerce & Traffic will receive increase,
And Merchants boldly venture when t'is Peace,

With Plenty fill'd, thy lofty Cities shine,
And all the Products of the Globe are thine.

Pub Augt 12, 1806 by I. Hinton 44 Wells Str^t. Oxford Str^t. London.

NOTE. Following the death of Pitt in January 1806, his government fell and was replaced by the so-called Ministry of All the Talents, headed by Lord Grenville and Charles James Fox. Throughout the summer of 1806 Fox entered into negotiations with Talleyrand with a view to agreeing a treaty. Ultimately these negotiations failed. The wording of the captions of these two pictures, nos. 67 and 68, expresses an expectation of peace rather than a celebration of its establishment. It seems likely that these pictures were published in the belief that the negotiations were about to achieve success. With their clear reference to the hope of the restoration of profitable trade they are interesting evidence of the economic burden on the country of the long French Revolutionary and Napoleonic wars.

68

No. 69 (large)

BRITANNIA, ſupporting the PROTECTORS of PEACE & LIBERTY.

London Pub^d. June 17. 1814 by P & P Gally 9 Turnmill Street Clerkenwell.

Notes. (i) Save for the different dates of publication and for some difference in colouring, this picture is the same as no. 64, but whereas no. 64 celebrates the Treaty of Amiens, this one must have been intended to celebrate the Treaty of Paris. It is the only example of one glass picture being printed for two purposes.

(ii) The 1802 version, no. 64, was published jointly by P. Gally and G. Stampa, but no. 69 was published by P. & P. Gally alone.

(iii) The short-lived Treaty of Paris followed Napoleon's abdication and banishment to Elba in April 1814: it was terminated by Napoleon's escape to France on 1 March 1815, resulting in the campaign which ended with his defeat at Waterloo on 18 June of the same year.

(iv) It seems likely that this picture and no. 70 were published in the belief that the Treaty of Paris marked the end of the long war with France.

(v) The significance of the figure 16 to the left of the inscription is not known.

BRITANNIA, supporting the PROTECTORS of PEACE & LIBERTY.

69

No. 70 (large)
BRITANNIA TRIUMPHANT and *PEACE* RESTORED

Sep 3 1814 Pub by J. Hinton 34 Charles St, Hatton Garden

© The Nelson Museum, Monmouth

NOTES. (i) This is the only glass picture the author has seen which celebrates both naval and military heroes, and contains the names of both Nelson and Wellington.

(ii) In addition to that of Nelson the flag on the left contains the names of the victorious admirals Howe, St. Vincent and Duncan, and of Captain Broke. On 1 June 1813 Broke, captain of the frigate H.M.S. *Shannon*, defeated the American frigate U.S.S. *Chesapeake* in a single-ship action off Boston. Coming after the defeat of three British frigates in similar single-ship actions in the early months of the brief war against the United States of America, the news of Broke's victory was greeted in England with wild rejoicing, reflecting more the extent to which British pride had been wounded by these previous defeats than the intrinsic importance of the victory itself. The inclusion of Broke's name in the list of illustrious admirals is of interest in that it reflects the disproportionate response to the destruction of one frigate. Cf. C. S. Forrester, *The Naval War of 1812* (1957), p. 146: 'It is not exaggeration to say that the adulation heaped upon Broke exceeded that which Jervis and Duncan received after St. Vincent and Camperdown … Broke was made a baronet, when even a knighthood was a rare reward for a successful single-ship action.' In this context it is to be noted that for his exploits at the Battle of St. Vincent Nelson received only a knighthood.

(iii) Published before the Battle of Waterloo; beneath Wellington's name the flag on the right contains the names of Beresford, Graham, Hill, Bow[…] and Fane, Wellington's officers; the fourth may be Capt. George Bowles, a friend of Wellington who was with him at Waterloo.

(iv) Even as late as 1814 the central flag, the Union Flag, is still incorrectly shown without the red diagonal of St Patrick within the white diagonal of St. Andrew: see no. 37, note.

(v) Published three months later than no. 69 and by a different publisher, J. Hinton not P. & P. Gally, in many respects this charming picture so closely resembles the earlier one as to suggest that it may well have been drawn by the same artist.

NELSON
HOWE
VINCENT
DUNCAN BROKE

WELLINGTON
BERESFORD
GRAHAM
HILL BOW FANE
&c &c

BRITANNIA TRIUMPHANT and PEACE RESTORED

70

APPENDIX I

Notes on Glass Pictures

The technique of making glass pictures was first described by Johannes Kunckel, in Germany, in 1669. The first description of the technique in English is to be found in the second edition, 1687, of *The Art of Painting in Oyl*, by John Smith, a polymath who wrote books on a variety of subjects. It is of interest that there is no mention of this technique in the first edition, published in 1676, suggesting that knowledge of the technique had not reached England at the earlier date.

In their *Treatise on Japaning and Varnishing* (Oxford, 1688), John Stalker and George Parker give a full account of the technique of making glass pictures. This account was reproduced almost verbatim by the Revd. William Salmon in the 8th edition of his *Polygraphice: or the Arts of Drawing, Engraving, Etching, Limning, Painting, Vernishing, Japaning, Gilding &c.*, published in London in 1701. Chapter XXIV of Stalker and Parker's book (page 73) begins:

To lay Prints on Glass

Having at large treated of the Colours, Oyls, and other materials required in this work; I proceed to instruct you how the Prints themselves must be laid on Glass. First therefore let your Prints be steeped in warm water flat-ways, for four to five hours, or more, if the paper be thick: provide then a thin pliable knife, with it spread Venice-Turpentine thin and even over the glass, and with your finger dab and touch it all over, that the Turpentine may appear rough. Next, take the Print out of the water, lay it on a clean Napkin very evenly, and with another press every part of it lightly, to suck and drink up the water of it; afterwards lay the print on the glass by degrees, beginning at one end, stroaking outwards that part which is fastning to the glass, that between it and the Print no wind or water may lurk and hide it self, which you must be careful of, and never fail to stroke out. Then wet the backside of the print, and with a bit of spunge or your finger rub it over lightly, and the paper will role off by degrees; but be careful, and avoid rubbing holes, especially in the lights, which are most tender: and when you have peeled it so long, that the Print appears transparent on the backside, let it dry for two hours; next, varnish it over with Mastick or Turpentine-varnish four or five times, or so often, till you may clearly see through it. After a nights time for drying, you may work on it.

To lay Prints, either graved, or Mezzo-tinto's, in such manner that you may role off the paper, and leave the shadow behind.

Soak the Print in water, dry it with a cloath, spread on the glass oyl of Mastick: and some Turpentine, and lay on the print upon it, exactly as before. When tis almost dry, brush off the paper with a brush, and you'l find none but the inky, shadowed part remain: then do this as the former with Mastick-varnish, which preserve dry and free from dust, until you are at leisure to paint upon it.

It is of interest that this account describes two methods. The first is clearly the quicker, and is essentially the same as that described in 1755 by a French painter, François Xavier Vispré, in a paper entitled 'Le Moyen de devenir peintre en trois heures…', and aimed at instructing young ladies to copy pictures by renowned artists without learning to draw themselves! In contrast to this rapid method, throughout the eighteenth century a number of descriptions were published which clearly took much longer than this, but evidence that glass pictures could be produced in only a few hours is a consideration of importance in relation to the Nelson commemorative pictures.

The first glass pictures in England were made from mezzotint prints of portraits, and the high quality of these pictures was essentially dependent upon the quality of the prints. In most types of print (such as engravings, dry points, etchings) the ink is held in the grooves formed in the smooth plate. In contrast, in mezzotint prints the surface of the copper plate is initially 'roughened to a texture similar to fine sandpaper, consisting of tiny troughs and peaks in the metal which between them hold a rich supply of ink – even after the plate has been wiped'.[1] The plate is formed by paring away and smoothing to a varying extent this roughened surface, the ink being held to a similarly varying extent. The surface of the plate was roughened by working over it with a tool with a curved, serrated, sharpened edge (a mezzotint rocker). To achieve a satisfactory surface the process was repeated in different directions forty times or more. The artist then worked on the

Figure E
ONE OF THE PRINTS USED IN MAKING A NELSON GLASS PICTURE
The glass picture is no. 41, above

[1] B. Gascoigne, *How to Identify Prints* (1986).

plate by smoothing away the fragile burr to a varying extent using a scraper or burnisher, the beautiful tonal variations of a mezzotint depending upon the depth to which the artist smoothed the roughened surface.

The finest mezzotint prints were produced in the middle years of the eighteenth century. Comparatively few copies of each print could be made, as the surface of the plate became blunted by the pressure of making the print; further, the preparation of the plates was time-consuming and expensive. It seems likely that it was these factors that led, in the latter part of the eighteenth century, to the use of simpler prints, less demanding in skill and time, in the making of glass pictures.

Some of the Nelson glass pictures, such as nos. 1, 2 and 3, were made from good quality mezzotints, but the typical commemorative pictures were made not from pure mezzotints but from mixed prints of an altogether different artistic standard. Copies of these prints are rarer than the glass pictures themselves, and the author has seen only two. Both, like the one illustrated (Figure E), are coloured. It is tempting to speculate that they were coloured as a guide to the relatively unskilled craftsmen who painted the back of the glass after the prints had been transferred to them: in fact there is no evidence in support of this supposition nor that the colouring was applied soon after the picture was printed. The prints are of great interest in that expert scrutiny of those that are available, together with study of the glass pictures themselves, shows that they are largely etchings, strengthened in places by some direct engraving of the plates, together with some light use of the mezzotint rocker. No doubt the extent to which these different techniques were used varied from print to print, but they were in all

Figure F
THE BACK OF A BROKEN GLASS PICTURE
(see above, no. 51)

respects simpler than fine mezzotints. Further, while the paper used for mezzotint prints was relatively thick, hand-made from linen or rags, the paper on which these prints were made was thin, machine-made, probably from straw or wood.

Figure F shows the back view of a broken glass picture, and Figure G the front view of the same picture. No. 51 in the catalogue is an unbroken example of the same picture. The crude nature of the oil painting on the back, requiring no great technical skill, is immediately apparent. It is not known exactly how this painting was done, but it seems unlikely that all the various areas of differing colouring could have been painted at the same time. Some areas must surely have been painted after the adjacent area was dry, when any overlap would not be seen from the front. Some of the modelling, such as that in this picture on the left side of Nelson's thighs, may well represent areas of light use of a mezzotint rocker on the plate. It is of interest that with a sharp blade the paint can be gently scraped away from the back of a picture, to leave the lines of the print still firmly bonded to the glass. The names of the artists who drew the prints are unknown.

The number produced of each of the Nelson glass pictures is unknown, though it must have been significantly greater than that of those made from high quality mezzotints. The technique used must have been essentially similar to that described above, no doubt using a relatively fast, robust technique for the transfer of the print to the glass by relatively unskilled labour. Following the announcement of Nelson's death in *The Times* on 7 November 1805, the first glass pictures were published a fortnight later, on 21 November.

Figure G
THE FRONT VIEW OF THE SAME PICTURE

APPENDIX II

The Death and Funeral of Nelson

This brief account of Nelson's death and the events culminating in his funeral in St. Paul's cathedral is included as a factual background to the events so dramatically – and in parts so imaginatively – represented in the glass pictures.

The first British ship to go into action at the Battle of Trafalgar on 21 October 1805 was the *Royal Sovereign*, the flag ship of Vice-Admiral Sir Cuthbert Collingwood, second in command of the British fleet (Nelson's 'my dear Coll'), which opened fire at 12 noon. Some twenty minutes later the *Victory* came under fire as, in the light wind, she slowly approached the combined French and Spanish fleet. At about one o'clock she broke through their rough line, astern of the *Bucentaure*, flag ship of the French Admiral Villeneuve. Raking this ship with a shattering broadside, the *Victory* turned to starboard alongside the *Redoutable*, the yard arms of the two ships becoming locked.

Throughout this period Nelson and Hardy were pacing the quarterdeck, side by side. A number of men armed with muskets were stationed on the deck and yards of the *Redoutable*, and at about 1.15 Nelson was struck on the left shoulder by a musket-ball fired by one of these men. Nelson fell to his knees, supporting himself with his left arm, saying as Hardy stooped to help him 'They have done for me at last, Hardy, my backbone is shot through.'

Nelson was carried down to the cockpit on the orlop deck, below the waterline. His coat, with all his decorations on the breast, and his breeches and stockings were removed, and he was examined by the surgeon of the *Victory*, William Beatty, whose examination revealed that he had indeed lost all sensation and power of movement below his breast, confirming that the bullet had severed his spinal cord, at that time inevitably a fatal wound. A little later Nelson said to Beatty 'You know I am gone,' to which Beatty replied 'My Lord, unhappily for our country nothing can be done for you.' Some ninety minutes after his injury Hardy paid the second of two visits, when Nelson bade him his famous farewell. The log of the *Victory* records, in an unknown hand, 'Partial firing continued until 4.30, when a victory having been reported to the Right Honourable Lord Viscount Nelson, K.B., he died of his wound.'

The following day Nelson's hair was cut off, as he had requested, and his body was placed in a barrel which was filled with brandy, secured vertically and guarded by a sentry. The *Victory* arrived at Gibraltar on 28 October, and five days later sailed for England, anchoring at Spithead on 4 December. On 11 December an autopsy was carried out by Beatty, who described Nelson's wound as follows:

> The ball struck the fore part of his lordship's epaulette; and entered the left shoulder immediately before the processus acromion scapulae … It then descended obliquely into the thorax … and after … penetrating the left lobe of the lungs, and dividing in its passage a large branch of the pulmonary artery, it entered the left side of the spine between the sixth and seventh dorsal vertebrae, wounded the medulla spinalis [i.e. the spinal cord] … directing its course through the muscles of the back; and lodged therein … On removing the ball,

a portion of the gold-lace and pad of the epaulette, together with a small piece of his lordship's coat, was found firmly attached to it.'[1]

On the same day (11 December) the *Victory* left Spithead for the Nore, with Nelson's body lying in a lead coffin in his cabin. On 21 December his body was taken from this coffin and after being dressed in a shirt, stockings and uniform small-clothes and waistcoat, neck-cloth and night-cap was placed in a coffin made from the mainmast of *L'Orient* (the French flag ship destroyed by the explosion of its magazine at the Battle of the Nile) and presented to Nelson by his captains at that battle. 'This was the last time the mortal part of the lamented Hero was seen by human eyes.'[2] This coffin was then placed in a leaden one and taken in 'the Chatham yacht' to Greenwich, where it lay in the Record Chamber of Greenwich Hospital until after Christmas.

Nelson's coffin lay in state in the Painted Hall on 5, 6 and 7 January 1806 (above, Figure B, p. 46). Enormous crowds came to Greenwich by water and by road to view the coffin. 'The number of people assembled in the town of Greenwich in the afternoon [Sunday 5 January] could not have been less than fifty thousand; and it is calculated that at least twenty thousand went away without being able to gain

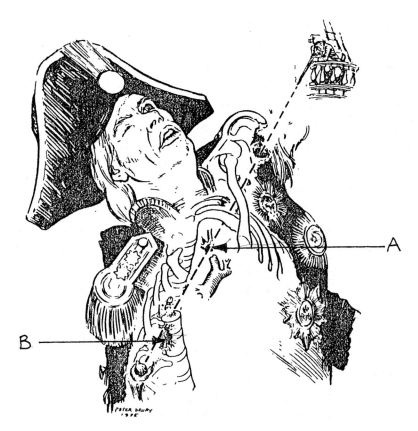

Figure H
DIAGRAM SHOWING THE PASSAGE OF THE BALL THROUGH NELSON'S BODY
A indicates the division of a major part of the pulmonary artery, and **B** the division of the spinal cord

[1] W. Beatty, *The Authentic Narrative of the Death of Lord Nelson* (1807), p. 70.
[2] Ibid. p. 78.

admittance.' 'The spectator could not behold the coffin of the departed without lamenting in the bitterness of sorrow, the fall of so great a man, and yet, when the word TRAFALGAR was presented to the eyes of the people ... they rejoiced in the victory.'[1]

On Wednesday 8 January the coffin was carried up the Thames in a magnificent water procession to Westminster. It was carried in Nelson's own barge from the *Victory*, pulled by members of the ship's crew (above, Figure C, p. 48). The river was closed to all other traffic, all the vessels moored in the river flew their flags at half-mast, and the banks were crowded with spectators. Included in the procession were the barges of eight of the City Companies, headed by that of the Drapers' Company, of which Nelson was an honorary freeman.[2] The banner flown on the barge of the Society of Apothecaries on this occasion can be seen displayed on the wall of the seventeenth century hall of the company. That evening Nelson's coffin lay in a small room in the Admiralty, in Whitehall, watched over by the chaplain of the *Victory*, the Revd. Alexander Scott. On the following day it was placed on a specially constructed funeral car drawn by six horses and carried in a great procession to St. Paul's Cathedral (above, Figure D, p. 51). The funeral service, attended by a large congregation headed by the Prince of Wales, started at 2 o'clock and it was dark as the coffin was lowered into the crypt. Later it was placed in a black marble sarcophagus, engraved simply HORATIO VISC NELSON, in the centre of the crypt.

---

[1] Archibald Duncan, *Life of the Late Most Noble Lord, Horatio Nelson* (London and Liverpool, 1806).
[2] Nelson's Funeral, reprinted from the *Gentleman's Magazine*, vol. 76 (1806).

INDEX

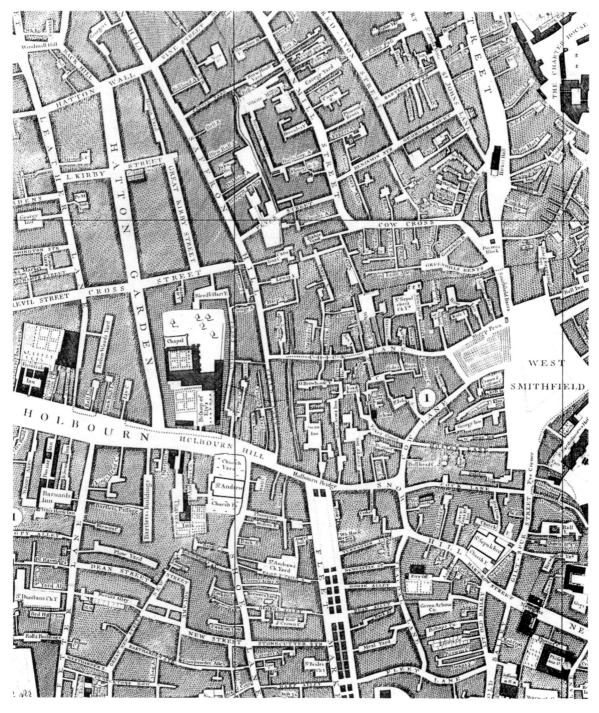

MAP OF THE SMITHFIELD AREA *c*.1800
© The London Topographical Society (see page 13 note 2)